Time Cops and Other Tales from the Criminal Justice Factory

Andrew J. Heller

Time Cops and Other Tales from the Criminal Justice Factory

FICTION4ALL

A FICTION4ALL PAPERBACK

© Copyright 2023
Andrew J. Heller

The right of Andrew J. Heller to be identified as author of this work has been asserted by the author in accordance with the Copyright, Designs and Patents Act 1988

All Rights Reserved

No reproduction, copy or transmission of the publication may be made without written permission. No paragraph of this publication may be reproduced, copied or transmitted save with the written permission of the publisher, or in accordance with the provisions of the Copyright Act 1956 (as amended).

Any person who does any unauthorised act in relation to this publication may be liable to criminal prosecution and civil claims for damages.

ISBN: 978-1-78695-909-6

Fiction4All
www.fiction4all.com

Introduction

There have been many, many memoirs by lawyers, particularly criminal defense lawyers. Some are written by (or ghost-written for) celebrity attorneys who have spent a lifetime promoting themselves and have become habituated to the limelight (for example, F. Lee Bailey); by others who are less-well known, but feel an overwhelming urge to write about some great injustice; by dedicated men and women with a noble cause to promote; by law professors, public defenders, Fortune 500 suits and Mafia mouthpieces (if those two are not the same); and enough miscellaneous others to fill the bookshelves of the main public library of a medium-sized city (Des Moines, Iowa.) The above list does not include the numerous works about famous trials, nor those about some particular aspect of the law or the legal system such as the death penalty. I would suggest of the overwhelming majority of these books, that if the last copies were lost in a fire, no-one, with the possible exception of the authors, would ever miss them.

Given such a hyper-abundance, even superfluity, of legal memoirs, it is incumbent upon me to justify my temerity in this collection of cases from my profoundly obscure legal career. Which is: of all the many books by and about lawyers and the law that I have read, I don't know of one that looks inside the courtrooms where the cases that don't get mentioned on cable news, but which constitute the great majority of cases in the United States, and are tried (or pled out) by poorly-paid lawyers representing run-of-the-mill clients.

Whereas criminal prosecutions are conducted by full-time government attorneys at the county, state or federal level, there is no such uniformity on the other side. Criminal defense attorneys range from the lordly nobility of retired federal judges and former Attorneys General whom only the wealthiest can afford, to the peasantry of neighborhood general practitioners, who rarely if ever are hired for a case more newsworthy than a DUI (Driving Under the Influence) or a local hothead charged in a bar fight.

Given that most criminal defendants are indigent (surprise!), and thus unable to hire a private attorney, the organization representing the lion's share of defendants are represented by the Public Defender, called the Defenders Association in Philadelphia and the Legal Aid Society in New York City. However, for a variety of reasons discussed herein, the Public Defenders must turn away many more cases than they can accept. Those who are not represented by the PD are provided with court-appointed conflict counsel by their local government, which is where I come in.

Practically all of my cases were court appointments, as they were for other attorneys like myself, who were obliged to labor at the bottom of the legal food chain. My friend Peter, an excellent lawyer who started out with the Legal Aid Society in Brooklyn, described court appointments this way: "We get the crumbs…," he would say, wriggling his fingers to suggest tiny objects falling through space, "…crumbs from the table."

Except where noted, the names of lawyers, defendants, witnesses, judges, *et al*, have been, in the immortal words of Jack Webb, "changed to protect the innocent," (by the way, was any suspect on *Dragnet* ever innocent?) This is to say nothing of protecting the far more numerous, not-so-innocent, persons mentioned herein and, not incidentally, to forestall any misguided defamation suits. Likewise, the times, dates and specific places named are not the ones recorded in the trial transcripts. This means that technically this book can be classified as "fiction." As an officer of the court, however, I cannot tell a lie, and I can assure you that everything in this book actually happened pretty much as described. That being said, I should add that I have taken the liberty of following the practice used in the television series *Law and Order*, by summarizing and/or skipping over the most tedious parts of the trials. You will therefore be able to vicariously enjoy the most interesting moments in these cases without the tedium suffered by the actual participants that constituted most of the process, such as sitting around a courtroom for half the morning waiting for a case to be called to trial, then having it continued to some date in the distant future. If you feel cheated by these abridgements and want to experience the real thing for yourself, just head down to your local county courthouse, find a comfortable bench in one of the courtrooms, and settle in for the day. I recommend that you bring a good, long book with you.

Most of my 30 years at the bar were spent as a court-appointed criminal defense attorney, and the majority of those in Philadelphia's Criminal Justice Factory... I beg its pardon..., I meant, of course, the Criminal Justice *Center*. Read on, and you will be rewarded with a view of our legal system from a perspective largely unknown to the general public: a rodent's-eye-view. I hope my readers will find the trials and anecdotes illustrating how the system works and how it doesn't, interesting and instructive. I also undertake to explain certain legal concepts when they arise in the course of a particular case. This will enable you to impress your friends the next time you find yourself discussing the latest legal difficulties of a celebrity or former President (no names, please.)

In the last decade, a few of the systemic injustices suffered by our poorest and least powerful citizens have been corrected (for example, the long overdue repeal of most of the draconian mandatory sentences for drug offenders.) On the other hand, while some light is finally being shed on persistent inequities such as the racism, abuse of power, violence and corruption endemic to many, if not most police departments, and the untroubled acceptance of these conditions by local district attorneys, as of this writing, these problems remain as resistant to change as ever. Perhaps this book will in some minuscule way encourage the institution of badly needed reforms. Let us hope that something does, because otherwise we may as well give up hope of ever having even an approximation of a fair criminal justice system in this country.

One:
The Time-Cops, or How Can You Be in Two Places at Once, When You're Not Anywhere at All?

Officer Ronald Johnson is testifying for the Commonwealth of Pennsylvania in the case of Commonwealth v. Gibbs, November Term, 1996, Court of Common Pleas Number 2103, the Hon. John J. Cheever presiding. "On the night of February 23, 1997, my partner and I were assigned to investigate community complaints about narcotics sales on the 800 block of Cambria Street," he says.

Johnson testifies like most Philadelphia narcotics cops: he rattles off his testimony as if it was a digital recording. I've heard this same prefabricated evidence almost word-for-word a hundred times before, with only the names, dates and places changing from one case to the next. My problem is how to convince jurors who haven't heard this stuff *ad nauseum* that police testimony like Johnson's rarely has much relationship to the truth, being primarily a product manufactured to get a conviction.

"I set up a surveillance in an unmarked vehicle at the northwest corner of Eighth and Cambria Streets, where I observed the defendant over there....," Johnson continues in an official-sounding monotone.

"For the record, the witness has indicated by point of finger the defendant Tyrell Gibbs, seated next to counsel," interjects Assistant District Attorney Carla Tallow. "Please proceed, Officer."

Johnson drones on. "I observed this defendant with co-defendant Raheem Phillips..." [Phillips is not here. His case was disposed of months earlier, when he pled guilty to three open drug cases including this one, in exchange for a 2 ½ to 5-year sentence to cover all three cases,] "...sitting on a stoop on the opposite corner from where I had set up my observation post. Approximately five minutes after I arrived, the defendant was approached by a young black male, who engaged in a narcotics transaction ..."

I am on my feet. "Objection. That is a conclusion," I say. "Suppose we let the jury decide what they were doing?"

If you haven't caught on yet, I am Gibbs' lawyer. I'll tell you more about myself later, but there's no time now. I need to concentrate on Johnson's testimony.

The judge looks down from the bench. He already appears to be tired of this case, and the trial has barely begun. "Objection sustained," he says with an air of strained patience. "Officer, please just tell the jury what you saw."

My objection and the court's ruling have derailed the witness's train of thought (if you can call memorized testimony from two hundred previous narcotics arrests "thought.") "Could you repeat the question, counselor?"

Carla helps the witness get his wheels back on the track. "What, if anything, did you see the defendant do?"

The witness nods, the needle drops back down into the right groove, and the playback resumes. "I observed this defendant accept a quantity of United States currency from an unknown black male, then go over to the stoop of a house at 801 Cambria, where an individual later identified as Raheem Phillips was sitting on the front steps. The defendant gave the U.S. currency he had received from the black male to Phillips. Then he removed a cigarette pack from under the steps, retrieved several small objects from it, and returned to his original location, where he handed the small objects to the unknown male. The male then left the area on foot, traveling north on the west side of Eighth Street. This happened at approximately…" Johnson consults his memo book, "…19:05…, that's 7:05 PM," he adds, for the benefit of those of us still using a 12-hour clock.

"And did you have an opportunity to make any other observations subsequently?" Carla's technique is not exactly polished, so sometimes her questions can come out sounding a little awkward.

Nonetheless, the Assistant DA's less than expert interrogation method does not throw the veteran Johnson off his game. He's been questioned less artfully than this before, and he's always managed to deliver his lines exactly as they were written in the script. "During the next hour, I observed ten similar narcotics transactions between the defendants and various buyers," he answers.

Ten! I think. Aren't we laying it on a little thick, Officer Johnson?

My client pokes my arm to get my attention. Without taking my eyes from the witness box, I shake my head and silently point to the legal pad and pen on the table in front of him. Before the trial began, I explained to Mr. Gibbs how important it was for me to watch the witnesses testifying and hear every word of their testimony, and I could not afford to be distracted. I told him that if he had something he wanted to bring to my attention while a witness was on the stand, to write it on the pad, and I would read it as soon as I had the chance. Generally, the client is about as sharp as a bowling ball, and thus unlikely to have anything useful to contribute.

While Gibbs scribbles away, I speculate about how the prosecutor will explain to the jury what looks to me like a big hole in her case. How, I wonder does Ms. Tallow intend to account for the fact that not one of these buyers was arrested, something I already know from the discovery? *I can't think of anything, at least not anything very plausible, and I doubt if she will be able to do any better. My guess is that she won't even try. I expect her to skate over and around the issue in her summation, telling the jury that the police never lie, so whatever her cops said *must* be true. This is a more or less standard tactic for prosecutors dealing with loose ends like this.

If the Assistant District Attorney expects Officer Johnson to clear the matter up for her, she is out of luck. He now has the bit between his teeth and is rampaging freely over the fields of his imagination. "The last transaction took place next to my vehicle. A black female approached the defendant, and asked him for 'two.' She gave the defendant a ten-dollar bill. He crossed the street, took two small clear objects from the cigarette pack, and handed them to the female," he says, looking at the jury. I am impressed by Johnson's ability to keep a straight face while telling such a blatant fib.

I don't know how these obviously fabricated observations are playing with the jury, but it requires an effort on my part to keep from shaking my head in disbelief. Does Johnson *really* expect the jury to believe that the drug dealer came right over to his car to make this sale, so that Johnson could not only see, but also hear the whole thing? Over the years, I have heard cops tell some mighty big whoppers on the stand, but this one is apparently bent on setting a new benchmark in prevarication.

"And what happened to the female?" Carla asks.

"She left the area on foot, eastbound on Cambria, and was not apprehended," answers the witness.

No kidding, I answer in my thoughts. We'll have to have a little talk about those sales on cross, Officer Johnson.

While Carla consults her legal pad to remind herself of her next question, I glance down to see what is on Mr. Gibbs' mind. He has written: "The police reports. Times crossed out?"

I look at Gibbs, and he touches the upper right corner on the 75-48 Incident Report, above the space for "time out," then then taps the "time out" box on the first page of the blue 75-49 Investigation Report. [The 75-48 and -49 are police forms generated by every arrest, and they usually constitute the most useful part of the discovery provided by the DA to the defense.] Sure enough, the original entries---which are supposed to record the time when the arresting officer left the precinct to go out on the assignment---have been struck out with a black marker on both forms and new times written in. The original times are still legible, however, and it is the same on both reports: 20:05 in 24-hour cop time (8:05 PM to you and me). In both cases the new time is one hour earlier, 19:05 (or 7:05 PM). I had noticed this during my trial preparation, but it didn't strike me as very significant at the time. Now however, I am starting to have second thoughts. Maybe it does mean something.

On the pad, I write "? I'll ask," and show it to the client. He nods, satisfied with his contribution to the case. Neither of us realize it at the time, but Tyrone Gibbs has just put his finger on the key evidence in the case I like to think of as "The Unusual Affair of the Time Cops."

My attention is drawn back to the witness stand, where Johnson has now rounded the far turn and is galloping down the homestretch. "At about 20:00..., 8:00 PM...I observed this defendant and Phillips enter a Chinese restaurant located on the southwest corner of Eighth and Cambria. I called in for assistance, and identified the defendants to responding officers, who placed them under arrest."

"Thank you, Officer Johnson," Carla says, sounding pleased with Johnson's evidence. "I have no further questions at this time."

The judge looks down at me from his seat high above me. "Do you have any questions for this witness, Mr. Heller?" He asks.

I stand. "Yes, Your Honor. If I may proceed?" I ask.

The judge nods. "Please do," he says.

This is a big moment in the trial. If I can't rough up Johnson on cross examination and knock some holes in his testimony, Tyrone Gibbs is probably going to be sent to stand in the corner for three to six years.

"Good morning, Officer Johnson." It makes a better impression on the jury if you are reasonably polite to the witness when you start the cross, and gradually work your way up to open belligerence.

"Good morning, counselor." Johnson says, nodding amiably.

I have some questions I am just itching to ask. The Commonwealth has (inadvertently I'm sure,) somehow neglected to ask Johnson what happened to all those buyers he observed, and I wouldn't want Ms. Tallow to be embarrassed when she realizes she had overlooked such an important matter. I assume she will be duly grateful when I cover for her oversight.

"Officer, you stated on direct examination that you observed eleven transactions in the vicinity of Eighth and Cambria, all involving my client, in which, you say, he received money from various people, and gave those individuals small objects in return, is that correct?" I am setting the stage for the fireworks to come (or so I hope.)

"Correct," Johnson answers stolidly.

"And as you have testified, you believed those transactions to be sales of illegal narcotics, didn't you?" I continue. As I ask this question, I walk away from the witness, to end up leaning on the rail at the far end of the jury box, so that the jurors are between me and the witness.

"I did," he says.

"Then, will you please tell the jury...," here I momentarily shift my gaze to meet the eyes of the fourteen good persons and true [twelve jurors and two alternates] occupying the jury box, "...what kind of narcotics were recovered from those eleven buyers when they were arrested, how the drugs were packaged, and whether the drugs and packaging recovered from those buyers matched the narcotics recovered at the time of the defendant's arrest?"

Like spectators at a tennis match, the jurors' heads swing back to Johnson as he answers, "There weren't any, counselor."

I do my best to sound surprised (in reality of course, I'm not at all surprised, since I already know this from the police reports.) I do a double-take, then repeat his answer back to him, "There weren't any...what? Buyers arrested, or narcotics recovered from them, Officer?"

"Neither, counselor. No buyers were arrested, so nothing was recovered," Johnson responds blandly.

Now I turn simulated surprise to simulated disbelief. "You didn't arrest *any* buyers...you *did* say there were eleven of them, didn't you?"

"Correct," he answers in a bland tone suggesting that he wonders why I bothered to ask. "There was no back-up available at that time to arrest buyers." From the expression on his face, it is clear that Johnson expects me, the judge, the jury and the rest of the world to accept this as a complete and final answer, and that as far as he is concerned, that is the end of the matter. If that *is* what he expects, he is in for a disappointment, as I am far from finished exploring this topic. Like John Paul Jones in his battle with the British frigate *Serapis*, I have not yet begun to fight.

However, for the moment, I switch to something else. "Officer, did you not testify on direct examination that you went to Eighth and Cambria that night to investigate citizen complaints of drug sales in that area?"

"Affirmative. When my partner and I received the assignment from the captain, he said..." he pauses, waiting to see if I will object to what his captain told him (technically, it's hearsay.) Since the entire purpose of this the question is to give the jury a chance to hear what the captain told Johnson, I do not object.

Seeing that I am not going to object, he finishes, "...that a local citizens group had been complaining to him..." (Not just hearsay, but *double* hearsay!) "... about the individual later identified as Raheem Phillips, who had been selling narcotics on the street at that location."

"So, is it fair to say that you went out to Eighth and Cambria expecting to see Phillips engaged narcotics transaction at that location, and that if you did see him, you intended to arrest him and whoever was working with him?" I plow on.

He mulls this question over for a second or two, probably examining it to see if it's some kind of trap. Deciding that it's safe to answer, he says "Correct, counselor."

Now that the pins are set up, it's time to roll my first ball down the alley. "Officer Johnson, you will agree with me that one of the common ways of proving that someone is selling drugs is observe these sales, arrest the buyers, then compare the type and packaging of the drugs found on the buyers with whatever has been recovered from the seller, which would constitute physical evidence of both where and from whom the drugs came. Isn't that right, Officer Johnson?"

He can hardly deny it, but he doesn't want to admit it to the jury, either. So instead of answering, "Yes," or "No," he tries to avoid answering at all. "No, not in this case," he says, no doubt hoping that I will be content with this evasion.

I am not so easily sidetracked, however. "No, Officer, please listen to the question," I persist. "In general, is that not one of the ways used by police to gather evidence of drug sales?"

"Yes," he concedes, "it's one way."

"Wouldn't the arrest of the buyers in an observation sale case like this provide objective evidence that the sales actually took place?" I ask. [In the specialized language of law enforcement, an "observation sale" means that the police stake out a location, watch a suspect and try to see him in the act of selling. In the other standard type of narcotics investigation, a plainclothes cop or someone working for police tries to buy the drugs the directly from the suspect. This is known as a "buy and bust."]

Johnson tries his non-answer again. "Not in this case, counselor."

"Officer Johnson," I ask, my tone a little sharper now, "didn't you even arrest the female buyer who you say you both saw *and* heard purchase narcotics from the defendant?"

"No buyers were arrested," Johnson is sticking with the one answer, no matter how many ways I ask, which, since he doesn't have anything better, is probably a wise decision.

"*Why* wasn't she stopped?" I snap. By now, I really am beginning to get fed up with his evasions and starting to lose my temper. "Did she open an umbrella and fly away?" I ask sarcastically.

"Objection sustained!" The judge doesn't even wait for Carla to get up on her hind legs to object.

I turn and walk away from the witness, taking a few seconds to cool off. I remind myself that the object of the exercise is to fluster the witness and make *him* blow his stack in front of the jury. I take a deep, soothing breath, and let it out before I resume the cross-examination.

"Well then, Officer," I say, turning away from the witness to face the jury, "perhaps you will show us the photographs and video recordings you made of all these drugs transactions you testified about on direct." The chance that he will do so is zero to several decimal places because, as we both know, there *aren't* any photographs or videos.

"I didn't take any pictures," Johnson says.

"No pictures?" I repeat. I turn to the witness, again speaking in a tone of mild disbelief. "Then perhaps you'll show the jury the..." [once again, nonexistent] "...video recordings you made of the defendant selling drugs *right next* to your vehicle."

"We don't do videos," Johnson explains, before I can ask why he doesn't have any.

"No videos either, hmm?" I muse aloud. "Let's see. You didn't arrest any buyers, and you didn't take any photographs or videos of the transactions. Other than your word, officer, what evidence is there that these alleged drug sales took place anywhere but in your imagination?"

"Objection," ADA Tallow jumps up. "Argumentative."

"Sustained." The judge looks down at me admonishingly. "Do you have any other questions, Mr. Heller?"

"Just a few, Your Honor," I tell him. As I resume the questioning, I note that Johnson is now eyeing me with what I take to be mild apprehension. "Well, Officer Johnson, since you didn't arrest any buyers and you can't show us any pictures, perhaps you can describe these individuals to the jury," I suggest. "What did the first buyer look like?"

I am taking a chance here, but I don't think it's a very big one. If Johnson can invent convincing details about these buyers, who I am fairly confident never existed, he may be able to salvage some of his lost credibility with the jury. I am not too worried about this possibility, though. If he was creative enough to make up those kinds of details in the middle of a cross examination, he probably would have put the invented descriptions into the police reports on the day of the bust.

"He was a young, black male, like I said," he answers. His uninformative response encourages me to continue this line of questioning.

"What was he wearing, Officer? How tall was he? Was his hair long or short?" I demand.

"He was a young, black male," Johnson says once again. He repeats the answer, with slight variations, sounding to me a little less sure of himself than he had the first few times he said it. "They were all young black males."

"What about the second buyer, Officer?" I continue to hound him, persisting as if I had not even heard his last answer. "Was he more or less than seven feet tall? Did he have an eye patch, a wooden leg and a limp? Was he carrying a parrot on his shoulder?" I hear a titter behind me from the jury box.

"Objection!" Carla Tallow leaps to her feet, coming to her cop's rescue. It's becoming obvious that the woman has absolutely no sense of humor.

"Sustained. The only description he has is 'young black males,' isn't that correct Officer Johnson?" The judge now extends a helping hand to the beleaguered witness.

Johnson, grateful for the help, agrees. "That's right, Your Honor."

"Do you have anything *else*, Mr. Heller?" the judge asks again. I get the impression that he will be unhappy with any answer but "no."

I'm not sure. I pick up the legal pad from the table and glance down at it, and am reminded of the crudely altered time entries in the police paperwork Gibbs pointed out. With no particular expectations, I pluck the police reports from the defense table, hand them to the court clerk, and say, "I ask these papers be marked as Defense Exhibits 1 and 2 for purpose of identification, and move them into evidence."

"Has opposing counsel seen these exhibits?" the judge asks.

"They are the 75-48 Incident Report and 75-49 Investigation Report, both supplied to me by the Commonwealth," I answer, holding up the flimsy blue forms for Carla to see.

She nods and says, "That is correct, Your Honor. No objection."

"Exhibits D-1 and D-2 are admitted without objection," the judge says.

"May I approach to show D-1 and D-2 to the witness, Your Honor?" I ask.

He looks at the prosecutor, who shrugs. Even if she wants to stop me from cross-examining Johnson on the police reports she can't, since he and his partner had prepared them, then attested to their accuracy with their signatures. You can almost always use a witness' prior statements to cross-examine him, especially if the statements have been written down or otherwise recorded, as they are here.

22

I go up to the stand, and offer the two reports to Johnson. "Officer, are these the 75-48 Incident Report and the 75-49 Investigation Report prepared by you in connection with this case?" I ask.

He glances briefly at the one-page 75-48 and the three pages of the 75-49. "Prepared by me and my partner, Officer Ralston, yes," he says, correcting me.

"And everything on these reports is true and accurate, is it not?" I ask.

"I didn't put down every single thing that happened, counselor," he protests.

"I didn't ask you if these reports were a complete record of this investigation, officer," I say. "I asked you if the information on these reports is, to the best of your knowledge, true and accurate."

He considers this, possibly seeking a way to avoid answering, but eventually concedes, "Yes, everything on the reports is true, as far as I know." [This is known in the business as making the witness "adopt" a writing.]

"Let me direct your attention to the block in the upper left-hand corner of the 75-49," I say, leaning over the rail of the witness box, and tapping the paper with my finger, "where the words 'time out' are printed. That's where you put the time you left the precinct to go out on this job, is it not?"

He shoots a quick sidelong look at me and does not answer right away. The wary, hunted look I noticed earlier has now returned. "That is correct," he says after a short, but significant, delay.

"You can see where the time was originally typed, 20:05, then was struck out, and 19:05 written in, on both the 48 and 49, can't you?" I ask.

"Yes, I see it," Johnson answers with what sounds to me like reluctance.

"Why were those changes made, officer?" I continue, not expecting much beyond a shrug and "I don't remember."

Instead, this seemingly innocuous question jolts Johnson as if he'd been goosed with an electric cattle prod. He sits up suddenly, thrusts his finger in my face, and bellows, "19:05 is the right time! I went out on the job at 19:05!"

I have been standing close to the witness stand, so I could point to the places on the exhibits I was asking him about. I am so surprised by his reaction that I take an involuntary step back. What could possibly be so important about the changes to the time on these forms, I wonder, that the question causes a major eruption? Whatever the reason, it's plain to see that Johnson *really* doesn't like being questioned about it.

Naturally, that makes me want to ask about it even more. "Who made those changes, Officer, you or your partner?"

Johnson has still not recovered from whatever set him off in the first place. He rises halfway out of his seat to say, "We both did, because 19:05 was the time we went out on the job!" He is remarkably emphatic about it, and his face is reddening visibly. The hope that he doesn't pop a blood vessel in the middle of my examination flits briefly through my mind.

"Then perhaps you can tell the jury why the *wrong* time, 20:05, was originally put on both the 48 and 49?" I am only mildly interested in his answer, which I do not expect to be very enlightening, but definitely want the jury to see the prosecution's main witness come apart at the seams before their eyes.

Johnson's response is all that I could ask for. Now looking and sounding more agitated than ever, he bellows, "I don't know how the wrong time got in there!" He is so loud that he wakes up juror Number 11, who had evidently dropped off at some point earlier in his testimony. "I just know that 19:05 is the right time!"

At this point, I judge that Johnson's performance is memorable enough to create a permanent impression in the minds of the juror, so I say, "I have no more questions for this witness," and let him go. When Johnson leaves the stand, he looks as if the ordeal of cross examination has left him a little unsteady on his pegs.

All the excitement has evidently taken a toll on the ancient judge as well, because as soon as I conclude the cross-examination, he rises and orders a twenty-minute recess. This gives everybody a chance to sneak off and catch a smoke before the Commonwealth calls its next witness. The Criminal Justice Factory is officially a no-smoking facility, but if you go outside to smoke, the slow elevators and courthouse security will make the round trip take a half hour or more, and you may be late returning to court. So, anyone who smokes, which includes most of the cops, and many of the lawyers, witnesses, and miscellaneous others, has to sneak into the stairway of the fire tower to satisfy his or her nicotine cravings. I have recently quit smoking, so I don't join them. Instead, I take advantage of the break to sidle over to the prosecution table, to see if I can obtain some additional police records from Ms. Tallow.

"Say, Ms. Tallow, don't they keep a logbook that the cops have to sign when they go in or out down at the precinct?" I ask.

She considers. "They have to sign a log when they take a vehicle out, and I think they keep another one at the desk, that they have to sign if they leave the precinct for any reason while they're on duty. Why?" she asks.

"I'd like see what time the logbooks have Johnson leaving the precinct on this job," I tell her. "I'm hoping it will clear up this business about the time on the 48 and 49."

She thinks about it, then says, "I can ask Sergeant Fontana. He was the desk sergeant that night. I subpoenaed him for today, so he should be around here somewhere." She goes out of the courtroom in search of Fontana.

My client tugs on my sleeve. "What's up with that cop? What you *do* to him?" he asks.

"I don't exactly know," I admitted, "but I have a few ideas. Something interesting may turn up."

I see Carla returning and go over to her table. "Well?" I ask.

"There's a vehicle log and a desk log," she says. "You want copies of the log pages from the day of this arrest?" When I nod, she says, "I can bring them in tomorrow morning."

"Thanks, I appreciate it," which I do. I probably could get this evidence without her cooperation, if I ask the judge to order the Commonwealth produce it, but it's also possible that he would deny the request. In any case, it's a lot easier for everybody if the lawyers to handle this kind of thing informally than it is to make a formal motion and argue it out before a judge. "And will you make sure that Johnson is here tomorrow, in case I think of a few more questions for him after I see the log entries?"

"Of course, he'll be here," Carla looks at me as if I'm stupid. "He's the arresting officer."

"Of course," I echo. "He'll still be making overtime." Cops tend to hang around all through a trial, if their superiors allow it. This includes officers who are only peripherally involved in the case and do not expect to testify. The ones who do testify will continue to loiter in the courthouse after they are off the stand, and often through jury deliberations, which sometimes can go on for days.

The explanation, as it is for so much of human behavior, is greed. I learned on my first job out of law school, when I was working for the DA in Kings County, New York (aka Brooklyn), that police are paid time-and-a-half when they work more than eight hours in any 24-hour period, a typical practice in unionized industries such as law enforcement. In Kings County, every arrest in the borough must be processed at the Early Complaint Assessment Bureau (ECAB,) and as there are a lot of arrests, there is always a long line of cops waiting to get their arrests written up. Some days, you could find cops at ECAB sleeping on desks, the floor, anywhere there was room to lie down, while they waited 6, 8, even 10 hours for an arrest to be processed. Naturally, they are on the clock all this time, and if an arrest was made near the end of their regular shift, every minute spent snoozing in ECAB racked up overtime. Whenever a Brooklyn cop needed some extra cash, at the end of his shift he would bust somebody for smoking a joint or committing some other minor offense, and go down to ECAB to generate some overtime. In October and November, when the cops were saving up for Christmas, there were so many of these arrests that the phenomenon was called, "Collars for Dollars."

The court crier herds us back to our places, and intones, "Remain seated while the jury returns to the courtroom." The fourteen good persons and true who hold Tyrone Gibbs' fate in their hands shuffle back to their seats in the jury box, and the Commonwealth resumes its case, calling Officer Jack Ralston, Johnson's partner, to the stand.

"Officer Ralston, were you working with Officer Johnson on the night of the incident that brings us here to court today?" Ms. Tallow starts him off with an easy one.

"Yes, I was. I responded to his call for back up to Eighth and Cambria, where I arrested the defendant Gibbs and co-defendant Phillips inside a Chinese restaurant at that location." His answer covers this question and the next one, which hasn't even been asked yet.

Carla Tallow is not put off by this mild case of premature explication. "Did you have the occasion to arrest anyone at that time and place?"

"Yes," Phillips answers. "I found the two defendants inside a Chinese store..." [this term is used to describe the small, all-night Chinese takeout eateries that cater to addicts, drug dealers, police and anyone else with a reason to be out late at night in the less desirable neighborhoods of Philadelphia] "... near the northwest corner of Eighth and Cambria Streets. At that time, I placed both defendants under arrest."

"When you say both defendants, who are you referring to?" Carla asks, ungrammatically.

"I am referring to the defendant seated next to counsel..." he points at Gibbs.

"For the record, indicating with the point of a finger, Tyrell Gibbs," Ms. Tallow interjects.

"...and Raheem Phillips," he adds. "They were both inside the Chinese store, apparently waiting for the food they ordered."

Carla now asks a leading question. "Did you recover anything from either defendant at that time?" I don't bother to object, but I mentally click my tongue in disapproval.

Ralston consults his notes. "From behind a waste can in the corner of the customer area, I recovered a clear plastic baggie containing 19 pink-topped glass vials. Each vial contained an off-white chunky substance later determined to be crack cocaine."

Once again, I don't object, even though the question is improper, as it both calls for a hearsay answer and lacks a foundation. Since there has been no evidence about either the vials he recovered or their contents, and Ralston didn't personally test them, his conclusion that they contained crack cocaine is technically inadmissible, at this point. However, since the contents of the vials were later tested at the police laboratory, and the results recorded in a laboratory report (no surprises: they were positive for cocaine base,) I would be in no position to dispute the evidence if the Commonwealth brought in the lab technician who performed the tests.

I had therefore made a pre-trial agreement with the prosecution (a "stipulation") as to the results of the laboratory report, so there's really no purpose served by objecting at this stage, when the evidence is coming in anyway. This, by the way, is just one example of the handicaps conflict counsel must overcome to do our job. A private attorney with a paying client can try to contest police lab reports, by hiring an expert who might find mistakes in the testing procedure, the results, or an investigator who might uncover intentionally falsified lab reports. Philadelphia County doesn't believe that indigent defendants or their court-appointed attorneys need expert witnesses, so they rarely if ever, authorize funds for them.

"Did you recover anything from Mr. Gibbs at that time?" The ADA persists in leading Ralston. I rise to object this time, but then think better of it and sink back down in my chair. The police reports say that one of the backups, Officer Wise by name, found a vial on the floor near Gibbs, but they do *not* say that anything was recovered from his person. I wonder if Ralston is suddenly going to remember something different than what is written in the 75-49. If he does, I should be able to straighten him out during cross-examination.

"No, I did not recover anything from Mr. Gibbs," Ralston admits, "but I later learned that Officer Wise …"

Now I am on my feet. "Objection."

The judge turns to Carla. "Is Officer Wise going to be available to testify, Ms. Tallow?"

"He's the next witness," she says.

"Then, I will sustain the objection," the judge rules.

"No further questions at this time." Carla says, returning to her seat.

I start off with something simple. "Good morning, Officer. You were partnered with Officer Johnson on this case, correct?"

"Yes," he replies.

"You left the precinct at the same time as he did?" I continue.

"I did."

"What time did the two of you leave the precinct on this job?"

"May I consult my notes, Your Honor?" Ralston asks, turning to the judge. The judge looks at me.

"I have no objection," I say. "Look at whatever you like."

"We left at 19:05, approximately. That's 7:05 pm." He says, after consulting his notes.

"Did you know that the 75-48 and 75-49 originally indicated that the time out was 20:05 or 8:05 pm, Officer?" I pick D-1 and D-2 from my table and begin to approach the witness with them. "If you need them to refresh your memory, Officer I have copies of those reports right here," I offer helpfully.

He waves me back. "I have my own copies right here." He consults his paperwork, shuffling the pages around rather longer than seems to be absolutely necessary, as if he is hoping to find that his version of the police reports says something other than what my copies do.

At last, the judge intervenes. "Perhaps you can point out the particular areas in the reports you are asking the witness about, Mr. Heller," he suggests.

This suggestion finally stirs the officer back into life. "Yes," Ralston says, as I again start toward the witness box to point out the time blocks on the police reports for him, "I see that the time out was changed from 20:05 to 19:05."

Now comes the key question. "Will you please tell the jury *why* the time changes were made?"

Ralston's reaction, like Johnson's, is most gratifying.

"Because 19:05 was when we went out on the job! We left the precinct at five after seven!" he explodes. "The other time was a mistake!"

So far, so good. Now for one other little matter. "When you initially took the defendants into custody, as you have already testified, were you alone or did you have another officer with you?"

"I was the closest to the scene when Officer Johnson called for back-up, so I was there first, by myself," he answers.

"And when you placed the defendants in custody, did you search them or pat them down for your own protection?" I already knew what he had done, because he had testified about it at a pre-trial hearing during a motion to suppress evidence. The jury hadn't heard this yet, though.

"I patted down both defendants," he replies.

"You didn't find any contraband on the person of Mr. Gibbs, did you?"

"No."

"You didn't get any contraband from Phillips either?" I persist.

"I recovered a bag of drugs from nearby ..." Ralston tries the old trick of answering the question he wants to be asked, instead of the one that was asked.

"Move to strike as non-responsive," I quickly cut in. The jury has already heard this testimony, so I'm not worried that it will hurt my case. The purpose of the objection is to highlight this moment for the jury, so that it will stand out in their minds during deliberations. Since I intend to refer to this testimony in my closing argument, I want to impress the jurors with the way the police witnesses consistently try to avoid answering certain questions, as if the trial was a game they were trying to win, rather than an attempt to find the truth. I am so accustomed to hearing cops dodge questions that I have to constantly remind myself that most people haven't been exposed to it, and aren't aware of it.

Many civilians believe that real police are like the ones they see on television, who never lie and always arrest the true criminal. They are often shocked and disgusted when they see policemen swear to tell the truth, then lie through their teeth.

"Sustained. The answer is stricken." The judge turns to the jury box. "The jury is to disregard the witness's last answer." To me, he says, "Next question."

"You didn't recover anything from Phillips, did you, Officer?" I will ask a question as many times as necessary, until I get an answer, and hope that the jury will remember how hard Ralston fought to not give one.

"No, I didn't recover anything from Phillips," he concedes, at last.

I wanted to clear up something else that was bothering me that. "Officer, you said that when you entered the Chinese restaurant, you were alone, and that you placed both defendants in custody yourself, correct?"

"Correct."

"You put *both* of them in handcuffs?" I repeated.

Now he hesitates. "I...I don't recall if I handcuffed both defendants right away," he answers.

That doesn't sound like the normal arrest procedure to me. What if one of the suspects was armed, or if he tried to attack the arresting officer before he was in restraints? "Well, there were two of them and only one of you. Wouldn't you normally handcuff both of them for your own protection?" I ask.

Ralston is not going to oblige me, for some reason. "I don't remember if I handcuffed both suspects."

I'm nothing if not persistent. "Do you remember if you handcuffed my client," I gesture toward Gibbs sitting behind me, "after you patted him down or before?"

Ralston is becoming monotonous. "I don't remember."

The judge tries to lend a hand. "He doesn't remember, Mr. Heller. Can we move on to something else?"

I have all I want from Ralston. "Thank you, Your Honor, I'm done. No further questions."

The judge looks up at the clock, then smiles down at the jurors. "I think we've done as much as we can for today, members of the jury. I'll let you all go now, and you all back here tomorrow morning at 9 o'clock." He stands.

The Court crier announces, "This Court is adjourned until 9 o'clock tomorrow morning. Remain seated until the jurors leave the room."

Day One of Commonwealth v. Gibbs is in the books. Now I can take a time out to tell you a little about my world and what I do.

Commentary: Public Defender or Not: What Difference Does It Make, Anyway?

As stated above, my practice consisted almost entirely of criminal cases, almost all of them court appointments to represent indigent defendants. Many people, including some clients, thought I worked for the public defender. This is a natural mistake, because the institution of public defender was created for the express purpose of representing defendants who can't afford to hire counsel.

But there is a very big difference between court-appointed counsel and the Defenders Association (as the PD is called in Philadelphia), one that is suggested by the second word its name: *Association.* The public defender in Philadelphia, like its equivalents elsewhere, is in fact an *organization,* a public service law office. This means that, although the PDs are notoriously underfunded, understaffed, and overworked, they still have support staff and other resources available to them that your average conflict counsel does not.

For example, the Defenders Association of Philadelphia employs full time private investigators, paralegals, social workers and has special units for appeals, juvenile law, and so forth. In addition, they have lists of expert witnesses willing to testify as needed, and the funds to pay them, which court-appointed counsel most definitely do not. (If a court-appointed lawyer wants to hire an expert witness, he must get authorization from the court, and assuming that court grants this request, he will usually find it next to impossible to retain a reputable expert for the amount of money authorized by the court.) Moreover, if the attorneys in the defenders' office tend to be young and inexperienced, it can at least be said of them that, the experience they *do* have is with criminal cases. In these ways, the public defender has it all over the court-appointed private counsel, and it is the lucky indigent defendant (luck*ier*, anyway), who is represented by the Defenders Association.

However, the PD cannot represent all of the indigent defendants; there are just too many of them. So whenever possible, the PD will raise a "conflict of interest," to have clients assigned conflict counsel, and avoid being buried under an avalanche of cases. These conflicts don't need to actually exist, they need only to *potentially* exist. One of the most common "conflicts" arises when multiple suspects are arrested and charged as co-conspirators in the same crime. This is the situation for many, if not most, poor defendants, because narcotics cases generate more than half the defendants, and almost all of them include conspiracy charges against at least two, and usually more persons. (This may no longer be true. After my retirement, Pennsylvania ran up the white flag and asked for terms in the War on Drugs. They srepealed most of the mandatory sentences for drug offenses, and now dispose of most narcotics case with non-custodial plea agreements, or so I understand.)

When multiple defendants are charged in a criminal conspiracy, the PD may represent only one defendant because the Rules of Professional Conduct---the ethical code for attorneys--- (and I'll thank whoever is snickering back there to control yourself, or you'll be asked to leave) ---strongly discourages attorneys from representing multiple co-defendants. This is because at some future time, one of the defendants *might* decide that he and a co-defendant have some hostile interest, as for example, if a defendant might testify against a co-conspirator.

That's why the Defender, who had been appointed to represent Raheem Phillips, asked the court to name outside counsel (me) for his co-defendant, Gibbs. If Gibbs, Phillips, or both decided to blame everything on each other, it would create a conflict of interest for an attorney who represented both me, that might prejudice the rights of the defendants. That was why I was representing Gibbs at trial, though by that time there was neither a co-defendant, nor any potential conflict of interest.

There are, in addition to the above example, numerous other types of conflicts and potential conflicts which the Defender by necessity, raises whenever possible. The foregoing, you will understand, is a very simple example. Those who want to learn more about this recondite subject should consult the PA Rules of Professional Conduct, Sec. 1.7.

Now, what kind of lawyer takes conflict counsel appointments? To begin with, he will most often be a sole practitioner or a member of a very small firm. This means that most of the time, she will not have a support staff of paralegals, research assistants, appeals units, social workers, etc., like the Defenders Association, underfunded and overworked though they may be. At most, conflict counsel will have a secretary and possibly a part-time law student for research.

In theory, a court-appointed attorney could hire a private detective to find witnesses, examine the crime scene, and generally investigate the case, but the fees authorized by the county for private investigators are so low that it was next to impossible to find a private detective willing to take a case. (PIs have to eat, too.) Of the few who would work for county rates, only one or two would actually do any investigating. The others mostly confined themselves to submitting vouchers for work they hadn't done, and were basically useless. Of course, this may have also changed since I retired, but I doubt it. I read the other day that court appointed counsel fees were finally raised for the first time in twenty years, so it doesn't sound like the courts have suddenly become generous since my day.

For most of the attorneys on the appointment list, criminal defense is a minor sideline. This is not to say that the attorneys on the court appointment list are uniformly incompetent. Indeed, some are excellent, experienced, and successful lawyers who feel a moral obligation to help at least a few of the overwhelmingly poor, black or brown individuals caught up in the criminal justice system. But as these lawyers still have to make a living, they can only accept one or two appointments a year, which has no real effect on the problem.

I did the work because (1) I could make a *modest* living from appointments, if I kept my overhead down; (2) I was completely independent, with nobody to answer to, other than my clients; (3) I took a considerable amount of pleasure from throwing a wrench into the gears of the justice machine that ground up so many people whose main crime was choosing the wrong parents, and being born in poverty; and (4) I thought the police acted as if the law was a game where they got to make the rules, that too many prosecutors were arrogant, self-righteous bastards who gave not a single damn whether the cops had lied or jiggered the evidence, and unhesitatingly prosecuted defendants who even *they* did not believe were guilty. I was also annoyed by judges who thought their job was to get a conviction, rather than seeing that defendants had fair trials. All of this got my back up. While I can't honestly say that all of my clients were innocent, or even that most of them were, the thought of standing around with my hands in pockets doing nothing while the Justice Machine ground them into sausage did not sit well with me.

My hero is the great fictional barrister, Rumpole of the Bailey, the creation of a real barrister, John Mortimer, Q.C. (Queen's Counsel.) Rumpole's entire *raison d'etre* is throwing wrenches in the gears of justice. Like me, he very much wants to win and abhors pleading guilty if he can see the faintest hope of victory. You might think that this attitude would be commonplace among members of the criminal defense bar, but in fact, many of my colleagues on the conflict counsel list were motivated solely by the money, which, since there wasn't very much of it, meant that were hardly motivated at all, and just went through the motions.

When I started practicing law in Philadelphia after three years in the Brooklyn District Attorney's office, I considered myself to be a decent attorney, competent, but far from brilliant, in other words, average. Over the years, as I had more opportunities to get to know my fellow conflict counsel and see them in action, my opinion changed, in part because trial experience made me a better lawyer, but mostly because I saw that the representation by most my colleagues fell considerably short of competent. In many cases, the word "abysmal" would be closer to the mark. I suspect that often their clients would have been no worse off representing themselves. Most of these attorneys were all too aware of their own shortcomings, and consequently applied their persuasive powers, not to juries, but to the clients, to get them to take guilty pleas.

So, what kind of representation did *my* clients get? Since I am now retired, and no longer constrained by the Rules of Professional Conduct, which forbids it, I am free to state my won-loss record, which was approximately 50 percent. Keep in mind that the great majority of criminal cases never go to trial. On average, 90 percent of all criminal cases are disposed of with plea agreements, 8 percent were dismissed, and only 2 percent go to trial. Of that 2 percent, how many times was the defendant found guilty? The correct answer is 80 percent. I have no way of knowing how well my fellow conflict counsel did at their trials, but given the above statistics, I think it is safe to say that my winning percentage was well above average.

As a trial lawyer, I was pretty strong in some areas, and not so much in others. I could usually see weaknesses in the Commonwealth case, I had a decent working knowledge of the Rules of Evidence, I could conduct a decent cross-examination, and in cases when I had a jury that was receptive to logical arguments, I could be moderately persuasive in closing. On the downside, I was not very diligent in trial preparation, relied too much on improvisation, and was much less persuasive in closing arguments where an appeal to emotion would have been most effective. So, I consider myself to have been a good, but not great, trial attorney. I daresay it would not have been difficult to find others with a different opinion at the Criminal Justice Factory, back when I was still practicing there.

Two: Time Cops, Part 2

The next morning while we are waiting for the judge to take the bench, Carla comes over to my table to hand me copies of the relevant pages from the two police logbooks. The desk log entry showed that Johnson had signed out at 20:01 (8 PM), and the vehicle log showed that he had checked out an unmarked van at 20:02. Most interesting! I thought, mentally rubbing my hands together. Oddly enough, Ms. Tallow did not seem to think that the log entries she had given me were of any importance. I suspected that she would have a different opinion before the trial was over.

After the last of the fourteen good persons and true of the jury finally finds his way back to the courtroom, the judge makes his entrance, the tipstaff calls the court to order, and the prosecution's case resumes. The Commonwealth's first witness is Police Officer Wise.

"Officer Wise," Ms. Tallow begins, "on the night of February 8, 1997, did you have any occasion to go to a Chinese take-out store at the corner of Eighth and Cambria Street?"

Wise looks down at the police notebook in his lap, which is, I presume, open to the appropriate page, then looks back up and says, "Affirmative."

"At what time did you arrive at that location?"

Again, Wise consults his notes, which under the rules of evidence, he isn't supposed to do without permission from the court, so I could object. But since I want him to get the time right, I am content to let him to recite his testimony from his notebook.

"At approximately 20:10, counselor," he says. "That would be 8:10pm."

"Now Officer Wise, will you please tell the jury what you did after you arrived at that location," Carla directs.

Once again, he consults his notes before venturing an answer. I conclude that Wise is either an unusually cautious belt-and-suspenders type, or has little faith in the reliability of his own memory.

"Once on the scene," he says, after he has assured himself that he actually had been present at the time and place in question and that his memory was not a hallucination of some kind, he looks at the jury and adds, "Upon my arrival, I was directed by Officer Ralston to take a suspect into custody and place him under arrest, which I did."

Carla waits a moment, no doubt expecting him to identify Gibbs on his own, but she is disappointed. Wise is clearly the kind of witness who doesn't volunteer any information beyond what was asked, so she is obliged to prompt him.

"And do you see that person anywhere in this room?" she asks.

Even though Wise's notebook almost certainly doesn't contain a picture of Gibbs, and thus will not help him to answer this question, I halfway expect him to check it again. Instead, no doubt reassured by the fact that a man is sitting at the defense table, and his tee-shirt and blue jeans rule out the possibility that he is the defense attorney, Wise points at Gibbs and says, "Yes. He's sitting over there next to counsel."

"For the record, identifying the defendant, Tyrone Gibbs," Carla says. "Now Officer Wise, did you recover any evidence in the course of this arrest?"

He peeks down at his lap, then says, "Yes, counselor. I found a glass vial with a pink top on the floor near where the defendant was sitting." He surprises me by continuing without being asked another question. "I placed the item on a property receipt and gave it to Officer Johnson, who was the investigating officer."

"Thank you, Officer Wise. I have no more questions," Carla finishes, resuming her seat.

"Mr. Heller," the judge says, "do you have any questions for this witness?"

"Thank you, Your Honor," I say getting to my feet. "I just have one or two."

"You may proceed," he says.

I start him off with an easy one. "Officer Wise, did you conduct a search of the defendant at the time of his arrest?" The police automatically and invariably pat down suspects when they take them into custody, so he could answer this one without consulting his notes, even if he had suffered total amnesia about this arrest.

"Correct. I patted down the suspect for my own safety at the time I took him into custody." Wise answers.

I expect my next question will call for another consultation with his notebook. "And did you find any contraband, illegal narcotics, weapons or anything else in the course of this search?" I ask.

When he looks at his notes this time, he evidently studies every word (which I guess couldn't be more than 50 or so) before answering, "No counselor, I did not recover anything except the one vial...,"

"Which was on the floor, a few feet away from the defendant, right?" I quickly add.

"That is correct," Wise agrees.

"Do you recall if you placed Mr. Gibbs in handcuffs, or if was he already cuffed when you took him into custody?" As this is not the kind of detail that would normally be recorded in a notebook, I expect Wise to say he can't remember.

But he surprises me. He stares up at the ceiling, pulls a couple of times on his lower lip to stimulate his memory, then looks at me and says, "Now that you ask, I remember that he had already been placed in handcuffs by Officer Ralston before I arrived."

I expect Carla to object here, as the only way Wise could have known who had handcuffed Gibbs was if Ralston had told him, which would be hearsay and inadmissible. But she evidently doesn't think it is worth bothering about, and lets it go.

The Commonwealth wraps up its case with the narcotics lab reports to which I have already stipulated, by reading them into the record, and publishing the bag of crack vials to the jury. (In this case, "publishing" means that the exhibit is passed around the jury box to give the jurors a chance to look it over.)

When the bag of crack is safely back in the hands of the court clerk, Ms. Tallow stands, announces, "The Commonwealth rests," and sits back down, wearing a smug expression that suggests that she thinks the case is safely home, dry, and in the barn.

"Mr. Heller, the Commonwealth has rested," the judge tells me, in case I had been suddenly struck deaf. "Will you be calling any witnesses?" It is plain that he does not expect the answer he gets, which is, "Yes, Your Honor, I would like to recall Officer Johnson."

Carla jumps up to object. "Mr. Heller has already had the opportunity to cross examine Officer Johnson yesterday," she complains. "What does he want to ask him today that he couldn't have asked then?"

The judge looks at her, then at me. "Members of the jury, there will be a very short delay while the two lawyers and I have brief discussion." To Carla and me he says, "Counsel will approach for a sidebar." We come around to the side of the bench furthest away from the jury box, to stand at the bottom of the steps leading up to the bench. He comes down to the last step, bends low over us, and hisses (to make sure the jury doesn't hear,) "All right, Mr. Heller, what's this all about?"

"Your Honor," I hiss back, "this morning I was given evidence proving that Johnson lied about when he left the precinct. These logbook entries..." I had the foresight to bring them up to the sidebar conference with me. I shake the sheets gently as I continue, "...show that he did not go out to Eighth and Cambria until just a few minutes before the arrest, and I want to ask him again why he falsified the time entries on the 75-48 and 49, because..."

"No," he cuts in before I can point out the significance of this evidence, "you are not going to recall this witness, because Ms. Tallow here is going to stipulate that Johnson went out at..." he pauses and looks at me, "...what time do these log books indicate?"

"At 8:02, less than ten minutes before the bust," I whisper, then try to resume what I was saying before I was interrupted, "which means that..."

I get no further before the judge once again intervenes, "Ms. Tallow will stipulate that Johnson left the precinct at approximately 8:02 pm, and that if he had been recalled to the stand and asked when he left the precinct, that would have been his answer. And that is the end of it. I am not going to waste any more time on this issue. You can both put your objections on the record, but my ruling is final."

From a purely legal point of view, the judge does not actually have the power to make such a ruling. While he certainly could have either sustained or overruled the prosecutor's objection (in fact, he was supposed to do one or the other,) and he had the power to decide if I could recall Officer Johnson for a fresh round of cross examination on this new evidence, the one thing he could *not* do was order Ms. Tallow and me to stipulate to this evidence, or indeed to stipulate to anything at all.

That's because a stipulation is an *agreement* between counsel that, instead of hearing testimony from a live witness, the jury will be given a summary of the stipulated evidence read to them by whoever is offering it. For example, when I agreed to forego testimony from a police lab technician that the glass vials contained cocaine, allowing Ms. Tallow to read the lab report to the jury, instead of calling the chemist to testify, that was based on a stipulation. But a stipulation only exists when both sides agree. A judge cannot *impose* a stipulation in a criminal case, because the Sixth Amendment of the Constitution guarantees a criminal defendant the right to confront and cross examine witnesses against him, while a stipulation, by definition, means that he will not be able to confront the witness, nor cross-examine him.

On the other hand, as a practical matter, I have no way to enforce Gibbs' rights, even though the judge's ruling violates the Sixth Amendment. All I can do is object to preserve Gibb's rights on appeal, and hope that the verdict will ensure that no appeal will be necessary.

The prosecution was actually worse off than the defense, in one respect, at least. If the judge commits reversible error, and the jury finds the defendant not guilty, the prosecutor has no right to appeal. Once a defendant is acquitted at trial, the Commonwealth cannot appeal the verdict, ask for a new trial, or ask for any other form of relief. Under the double jeopardy clause of the Fifth Amendment to the Constitution, it is forbidden to try a person more than once for the same crime.

In any event, it is clear that the judge is not going to change his mind, and I can forget all about eviscerating Johnson on the witness stand with the logbook entries. I will just have come up with a creative way of presenting this evidence in my summation.

The judge summons the court reporter, who records a whispered summary of the arguments of counsel (the judge's version of them,) and his ruling, after which Carla, then I, mutter our objections into the record of the trial. The judge motions us back to our places, resumes his seat on the bench, bangs his gavel to awaken any jurors who may have dozed off during the sidebar conference, and says, "Members of the jury, you will recall the instructions I gave you a few minutes ago about stipulations, just before Ms. Tallow read the police laboratory reports to you, so I don't see any need to repeat them. Instead, I am just going to read a stipulation between the two lawyers concerning Officer Ronald Johnson, who you will recall testified yesterday. Instead of calling him back to the witness stand, counsel have agreed that if Officer Johnson was asked under oath what time he left the precinct on this case, his answer would be 8:05 PM."

He looks meaningfully at Carla, then at me, and asks, "Is it so stipulated and agreed?" in a tone that implies that anyone who disagreed would soon come to regret it.

"So stipulated," I repeat after Carla, as unenthusiastically as she.

"Good," the judge pronounces, obviously well pleased with his clever disposition of this potentially time-wasting issue. "Now, Mr. Heller, I will ask you again: do you wish to present any evidence for the defense?"

"Your Honor, I would ask for the photocopied pages from a police desk log and a vehicle log which show that Officer Johnson signed out of the precinct at 20:02 hours, be marked as Defense exhibits 3 and 4 and move them into evidence…They were given to me by Ms. Tallow this morning, Your Honor," I add, in case she decides to make any difficulties about admitting this evidence.

"Does the prosecution have any objection to the admission of exhibits D-3 and D-4?" The judge asks Carla.

She doesn't answer right away, and I suspect the delay is because she is trying to think of a reason to keep it out. So does the judge, who asks, "Is there any reason to question the question the accuracy or reliability of this evidence, which *you* supplied to counsel?"

She can't give him a reason, because there isn't one, so she shakes her head, and says, "No objection."

The judge's head swings back to me again. "Does the defense have anything else?" He asks.

"No, Your Honor, the defense rests," I answer.

"Both sides having rested," he says, swiveling his chair to face the jurors, "the evidence is now closed, and we will proceed to closing statements after lunch." He glances at the clock on the back wall of the courtroom. "We will adjourn until two o'clock." He stands, the court officer commands, "All rise," whereupon, lawyers, jurors, court staff and judge scatter to the four winds, hoping no doubt that a good lunch will help them to survive an afternoon listening to long, tedious speeches by the lawyers, followed by even duller instructions from the judge.

Commentary: Judge or Jury?

In Pennsylvania, as elsewhere, a criminal defendant charged with a felony has the option of being tried by a judge and jury, or by a judge alone (this is known as a "bench trial".) The difference is that, in the former, a jury determines the facts, while the judge decides only the law of the case; while in the latter, the judge performs both functions. The main advantage of the jury trial for the defendant is that, in general, he has a better chance to be acquitted, assuming his lawyer is halfway competent and he has any kind of case at all. The advantage of the latter is that the trial is much quicker, which primarily benefits the defense attorney, prosecutor, and the court system, but hardly ever the defendant. This is because, as noted elsewhere in this book, judges -- whether consciously or otherwise -- tend to favor the prosecution, often to a degree that a bench trial before certain judges is known colloquially among the defense bar as "a slow guilty plea," (for an example, see Chapter Seven.)

This was one reason I almost invariably advised my clients to take a jury. But it was not the only reason; there was another, less worthy reason, as well. To explain, I will have to take you on a brief detour.

Until 1995, court-appointed counsel in Philadelphia were paid on an hourly basis. At the end of a case, the attorneys would prepare a "fee petition" detailing the dates, hours, and work performed in the course of representation. The fee petition would then be presented to the court for payment. The rate of compensation was a rather paltry $25/hour for out-of-court work (such as trial preparation,) and $40/hour for in-court. You will understand that these rates did not tempt many practitioners to participate in the court appointment system, especially if they had substantial rent and other overhead to meet. Even for the downtrodden masses like myself and my fellow conflict counsel, the income we made from appointments was not enough to keep body and soul together, particularly if we were overly scrupulous in the billing on our fee petitions. In order to survive, we were obliged to add a few hours here and there to fatten up the final totals. This was understood by all parties involved -- including the judges who were supposed to review these petitions before approving them -- because if the fee system was strictly policed, there might well be no conflict counsel at all. In any case, it was impossible to know what the real figures were, since the court had no way to keep track of how much out-of-court prep time the lawyers were actually devoting to their cases.

The system had other disadvantages as well. It was cumbersome and time-consuming, as each individual fee petition had to be reviewed and approved by the assigned judge. The process was also painfully slow: it typically took six months to a year before we finally received our lamentably small fees. As a result, calls for reform of the fee compensation system were regularly made by both judges and lawyers. Still, nothing was done, because it seemed to the Powers That Be that the work required to fix the system would be more trouble than it was worth, and in any case, nobody gave a rat's ass for the problems of legal bottom-dwellers like conflict counsel.

That all changed in 1995, as the result of the actions of one man, an attorney who, like Edgar Allen Poe's "rare and radiant maiden," shall remain nameless *here* for evermore. Let's just call him M (for M-bezzler). M decided that since he was going to lie about his hours on the fee petition anyway, he might as well go all in. Not for him the additional 15 minutes here, the extra half-hour there: he would take the court for some *real* money.

And he did so very successfully for two years before anybody noticed the unusually large number of hours he was billing, although it is difficult to see how some of the anomalies could have slipped through the cracks. For example, M billed for 12 hours of in-court time on New Years Day, a most unusual day for a court to conduct business. He was even busier on days when the courts were actually open, billing in excess of 24 hours a day on numerous occasions. The result was that while, other conflict counsel, such as yours truly, were making perhaps $25-35,000 annually from court appointments, our enterprising colleague raked in over $100,000 in the first year of his scheme, and more than $150,000 in the second (and last.)

M's crimes were eventually uncovered by a local reporter, and the story ran on the front pages of the *Philadelphia Inquirer* for a week, subjecting the broken, corrupt pay system to the pitiless light of publicity, and leaving the city officials charged with its administration no choice but to, at long last, set about instituting reforms.

One reason M was able to skin the city on such a grand scale was that he took the precaution of splitting up the 26, 30, or whatever number of hours he allegedly worked in a particular day into numerous petitions, none of which were submitted to the same judge. (I'm not sure this refinement was absolutely necessary. If anybody had actually looked at M's billables, he probably would have become at least a *little* suspicious, when he saw that M was charging for court appearances on Christmas, New Years, and other holidays when no court was in session.) So, a new Counsel Fee Office was set up, where all petitions for counsel fees would be filed together with all fee applications by each individual attorney. Thus, if someone was running up unusually big charges, it would presumably be spotted right away.

But the issue of attorney preparation time remained. There was no way to know how much time the attorneys were actually spending getting their cases ready for court, short of placing optic and audio bugs in their offices, a practice that would be almost certainly be frowned upon by the higher courts, to say nothing of the lawyers. The solution was both simple and brilliant: they decided to dispense with keeping track of prep time altogether. Under the new system, court-appointed counsel would receive a flat fee for *all* out-of-court work, and a *per diem* rate for trials. The prep fee for misdemeanors was set at $200, for felonies at $600, and for homicides, a munificent $1500. Trial compensation was $100 for a half-day or less (up to three hours,) and $200 for a full day. Thus, at a stroke, the hourly fee petition became as extinct as the dodo.

The new system made almost everyone involved happy (well, happ*ier*,) as it both increased compensation for the lawyer, and simplified the processing of counsel fees. Moreover, the decreased paper shuffling made everything more efficient: counsel fees were now expected to be paid only a *month* after the papers were filed, and (sometimes) they actually were! The revamped counsel fees system was such a vast improvement on the old hourly method, that Philadelphia's model was soon adopted by other big-city jurisdictions, who had been using the same antiquated system as pre-reform Philadelphia, and had been suffering from the same problems. For all this, we can thank the boundless greed of one man: M.

Which brings us back (finally) to the second reason for my strong preference for jury trials: *money*. A jury trial almost never lasts less than two days, and usually takes at least three. In addition, there are usually pre-trial motions to argue, such as motions to suppress evidence or statements, which can often take a full day by themselves. Then there's the jury selection process which, if the judge allows the attorneys leeway to question the prospective jurors thoroughly, can take another day, or even longer, especially if there are co-defendants. Nor is the trial itself free from all sorts of interruptions. The judges are obliged to take time out to dispose of other cases on their list, usually by continuing them, but sometimes they must stop completely to take care of some absolutely necessary matter, such as a Violation of Probation/Parole hearing, or sentencing a defendant from an earlier case who had been brought down to Philadelphia from state prison for this purpose, or any number of other things. Also, the jury may have to be sent out of the courtroom while the attorneys argue over the admissibility of some proffered testimony, or whether a certain piece of evidence should be accompanied by a warning or instruction from the bench and the wording of that instruction. Then there are the closing arguments and charging the jury with the applicable law, which can eat up another few hours. And while all this was going on, I was collecting 200 smackeroos a day, a circumstance that gave me a wonderful, warm feeling all over.

I should note that, while a lengthy jury trial was the ideal outcome for a court appointment, it was exactly the opposite for a private attorney, who normally is paid up front, and could not look forward to extracting additional money from the client, no matter how long the trial dragged on. For these practitioners, the best result is a plea bargain, which disposes of the case in the shortest time. Next best is a bench trial and, particularly in cases where there really isn't much of a defense, private attorneys try to persuade their clients that it is in their best interest to take a bench trial, rather than a jury. This, of course, does not apply to the high-profile defendants who make the evening news, since it is in these cases that the big-name attorneys make their reputations.

Since we're on the subject of juries, this would be a good place to share a story illustrating the importance of jury selection. It was told to me by a distinguished member of the bar, who was at one time the head of the Trial Lawyers Section of the Philadelphia Bar Association, so if you find it objectionable, blame him for leading me astray.

There once was a goat farmer who took the term "animal husbandry" too literally. Not to put too sharp a point on it, he frequently enjoyed carnal knowledge of certain members of his flock. After many years of this unappetizing practice, he was caught in the act and arrested. He went immediately to his family lawyer, and told the latter the entire story.

The lawyer said, "Well, you're in a tough spot. I certainly can't do much for you. But I can recommend someone. If anybody can help you, he can. *He* knows how to pick a jury."

The farmer went to see the new attorney, and once again, laid out his story. The attorney listened, and when the farmer was done, he said, "You've come to the right place. There's not another lawyer in the county who could win a case like this. Just make out a check for $50,000 for my retainer, then sit back and relax; your troubles are over."

The farmer was outraged by the fee. "$50,000?" He repeated. "How can you possibly charge that much?"

The lawyer smiled. "Because *I* know how to pick a jury. Now, do you want to pay my fee, or would you rather spend the next 5 to 10 years in the state penitentiary?"

The framer grumbled some more, but eventually saw that the money would be no use to him in prison, so he wrote out a check, ripped it from his checkbook, and slammed it down on the attorney's desk. "For this kind of money, you'd better get me off." He declared.

"Don't you worry," the attorney said. "You're as good as acquitted. I told you; *I* know how to pick a jury."

Six months later, the trial is underway, and the prosecution's star witness is on the stand.

"Please tell the jury, in your own words, what you saw that brings you to court today," the prosecutor says.

The witness, an Amish woman of a certain age answers, "It was the most horrible thing I've ever seen. That *man*..." she points a trembling finger at the defendant, "...was standing behind a young goat, with his pants down around his ankles. He had a hold of the poor animal, and he was..." She stops, overcome with emotion. "I can't say it. It was too terrible to describe..."

"Please try," the prosecutor urges. "The jury wasn't there, so you'll have to tell them what you saw."

With this encouragement, the witness proceeds to describe the defendant's actions in detail, indeed, with a certain relish. "...and at the very end he did the most disgusting, perverted thing of all. By the time he was finished, the goat had collapsed to its knees. He went around to the front, held the poor beast's head up and made the goat lick him clean!"

Juror Number One nods, turns to Juror Number Two and says, "A good goat will do that."

Snapshot: A Day at the Plant

Even on a slow day down at the justice factory, there is always the possibility of some innocent fun. Today, I have just returned from town, where I persuaded a client to plead guilty to a charge of Receiving Stolen Property (RSP) a 3rd Degree Felony, if the property is a motor vehicle, in this instance, a 1998 Acura Integra.

Normally, I do not advise clients to take guilty pleas if I can see any realistic hope of winning a trial. In this case, however, any possibility of successful defense disappeared when the owner of the car showed up to testify. The facts in brief are as follows: the car was stolen from Newark, Delaware on December 7, 2006. Because it was equipped with a LoJac ™ stolen car recovery beacon, the police were able to trace it, and five days later, the car was found by the police in a garage in Northeast Philadelphia. The police did not have to enter the garage to identify the stolen Acura, which was just as well, since they didn't have a search warrant. However, the car was clearly visible through the windows of the garage, which the owner had carelessly neglected to cover. After identifying the car, the police got a search warrant for both the garage and the house it was attached to, and conducted a search of both. In the garage, along with the stolen Acura, the police found a pair of doors taken from another car of the same year, model and make. The VIN (Vehicle Identification Number) on these orphan doors had been scratched off, as had the VIN for the Delaware car. Inside the house, they found my future client, Mr. Julio Rodriguez, and his girlfriend, as well as some photographs of him. One of the photographs depicted Rodriguez sitting in the Acura.

Mr. Rodriguez insisted that he was innocent of any wrongdoing. He had no idea, he told me, that there was a stolen car in his garage, and yet, he could offer no explanation for how it could have gotten into the locked garage. Nor could he think of anyone who might have played this prank on him. Likewise, the source of the photographs the police found in the house was to him a mystery as profound as that of the meaning of the universe.

I had the above conversation with Mr. Rodriguez at the Detention Center, where he was lodged awaiting his court date, and at the end, I recommended he take the plea offer of RSP and a sentence of 11½ to 23 months in county jail. Initially, he wanted to fight the case, insisting, as set forth above, that he was a victim of circumstances and as innocent of wrongdoing a newborn babe. After I pointed out that, in addition to the above evidence, he had two prior convictions for Receiving Stolen Property in the form of stolen cars and parts stripped from stolen cars, which would probably mean a state sentence if he were convicted at trial, he agreed that the plea was the better option.

While we waited in the courtroom for the judge to take the bench, I flipped through the pictures the police had taken from the house. As I write this, I'm looking at them to refresh my memory.

The first one shows my client with his right arm around his girlfriend's shoulders, while he holds a baby in the crook of his left arm and a fanned-out wad of cash consisting of approximately fifty $20 bills and a few $100s in that hand.

In the second photo, his girlfriend is not visible. He now holds the cash in his right hand, and the baby on the left. In this shot, the photographer has captured an excellent view of the large dragon tattoo on his left shoulder.

The third and last photo is the best of the lot. Mr. Rodriguez is posed flopped in a beanbag chair with his legs spread wide and his hands behind his head. He is stripped to his underwear (you can read the "Hanes" label on the waistband), giving us an opportunity to admire his superb physique: shapeless mounds of pale flesh decorated with ample quantities of dark, curly hair. His state of *deshabille* also allows us to appreciate another tattoo, this one consisting of the word "Malante" (a Spanish word meaning "criminal" or "evil",) written in Old English script across his bulging abdomen. A number of other tattoos on his chest and forearms are also visible, but sadly, are too blurry in the photo to show any detail. Resting against his right thigh is a bottle of Jose Cuervo Black; against the left, a bottle of Absolut Vodka. The cash is now tucked halfway into the waistband of the aforementioned briefs. I reflected that these photos would have made a wonderful impression on the jury, had we gone to trial.

An ADA who was there on another case noticed the pictures of Mr. Rodriguez and came over to look at them. Indeed, it would not be an exaggeration to say that she could not take her eyes off the three photographs, especially the last. When one of her colleagues who also had a case in the room came in, she insisted I show him the pictures from the file.

"Come over here," she said, "and look at these great pictures of my boyfriend."

Three: Time Cops Part 3

The lunch recess gives me time to get over my pique at the judge's ruling, and somehow emphasize in my closing statement the importance of testimony the jury did *not* hear from Officer Johnson's mouth in a way that would make a real impression on them. By the time the crier signals the return of Judge Cheever by announcing "All rise," I think I have one.

The judge settles his bottom on his chair, turns to the jury, and says, "Members of the jury, as I said before we broke for lunch, this is the opportunity for opposing counsel to make their closing arguments. Mr. Heller, as counsel for the defendant, may if he wishes, choose not to make any statement at this time. I remind you that the defendant has the right to remain silent, and you cannot hold it against him."

Now he looks in my direction. "Mr. Heller, will you be making a closing statement on behalf of Mr. Gibbs?" He asks.

"Thank you, Your Honor, yes, I will," I say, standing, moving around the table to head for the jury box.

"Members of the jury, I suspect that like me, you had unanswered question about a number of things Officer Johnson testified to yesterday." I want the jurors to feel as if they are thinking along with me, unraveling the mysteries of the case together.

"Why couldn't he describe *anything* about the ten persons who he said he saw buy narcotics from

Mr. Gibbs, other than 'young, black males?' Even if he has an unusually bad memory, he could have jotted some descriptions of them down in his notebook at the time. Then there's another question: when he went out to Eighth and Cambria to investigate drug sales there, why didn't Johnson bring along a couple of backup officers to arrest the buyers? The whole purpose of the investigation, after all, was to gather objective, physical evidence that the suspect was selling narcotics, and if drugs were recovered from these buyers, that would provide this evidence, especially if the packaging and contents were the same as what was found in the suspect's stash. He didn't want to, but Johnson admitted that is the standard procedure for this kind of investigation."

I pause to see if I have their attention, and it looks like I do, so I go on. "Now we come to the strangest part of all: the business with the changed time on the two police reports."

To the court clerk, I say, "May I have Exhibits D-1 and D-2, please?"

The clerk takes them from a manila folder, and hands them to me. I hold up the 75-48 Incident Report to the jury, and say, "If you look at the upper right corner, you can see where someone drew a black marker through the time originally written there, but you can still read it: 20:05 or 8:05 pm, and wrote in 19:05, which is 7:05 pm."

Now I display 75-49 to the jury. "And you can see that the same thing was done in the 'Time Out' box of this Investigation Report," I continue, holding the blue paper at the top, so that my forefinger is just above the part of the report I want them to look at. "Again, the original time, 8:05 was blacked out, and 7:05 written in below. Take a look for yourselves."

To the judge I say, "May I publish these exhibits to the jury, Your Honor?"

He nods and answers, "Go ahead."

As the police reports are passed along, I watch the jurors, to see how much interest they show in these exhibits. It seems to me they all took a good, long look and that one or two scrutinize them for an extra few seconds.

When the exhibits complete their circuit around the jury box and are returned to the clerk, I pick up the thread again, "It could, I suppose, have simply been a mistake, a minor clerical error. Somebody's watch was fast, or something like that. I confess that I didn't think it was particularly important, either..." I look over at the prosecutor to see how she is taking in my closing statement. She looks unconcerned, even a little bored. I guess I haven't made much of an impression on her so far. I suspect she will soon become more interested shortly.

"...until yesterday, when Johnson and his partner Ralston both erupted like volcanoes, when I asked them why the time on the reports had been changed. I'm sure you remember the way Johnson yelled, turned red, and *insisted* that he left the station at 7:05, and definitely *not* at 8:05."

Judging from their faces, they remember it all right. A few nod their heads in agreement.

"And Ralston, he was just sure as his partner. He acted the same way when I asked him those questions, and just like Johnson, never explained why the time had been struck out and changed. Obviously, they both thought it was important, and it is equally obvious that they didn't want *you* to know why it was done."

I walk down to one end of the jury box (until now I've been standing halfway down), then say, "So I put on my thinking cap during the lunch break, and after a little thought, I came up with what I believe is the explanation. Actually, I thought of two possibilities. One is that Johnson went over to Eighth and Cambria at 8 o'clock, didn't see anybody selling drugs, so he back to the precinct, hopped in a time machine and traveled back an hour to 7:05, then out to the location again to observe all the sales he testified about…"

I pause momentarily, to allow a wave of partially suppressed giggles by some of the jurors to pass, then go on. "But since the Commonwealth didn't introduce any time-travel evidence, that conclusion would be based on unsupported speculation, and as the judge will tell you when he instructs you on the law, you may not find the defendant guilty based on mere speculation; the verdict must be supported by evidence. That leaves the other explanation: that Johnson never saw any narcotics sales at all, because he wasn't there long enough to see anything. Because he went out to Eighth and Cambria a few minutes after 8 o'clock, and the moment he saw my client and Phillips at the Chinese take-out joint, he called in his back-up to arrest them. Johnson already knew who he was looking for… you will recall that the captain had passed on the complaint from the neighborhood watch... and he was in too much of a hurry or too lazy to do any actual investigating. He probably expected the arresting officers to find drugs on the defendants, but when he got back to the station house, he found out that nothing had been recovered from either one, and all that was recovered was the bag of 19 vials found behind a trash can in the Chinese store, which couldn't be connected to anybody."

The jurors are definitely listening now. I take a quick glance at Carla out of the corner of my eye. As I had predicted, she's now paying a lot more attention than she had been a few minutes ago.

"Now, Johnson and Ralston are veterans, and they knew they needed something to link the 19 vials recovered in the store to Gibbs and Phillips, like some drug sales, for example. They needed to create some evidence, or Johnson's inexcusably shoddy investigation would be exposed." I stop here and look each juror in the eye. "And that is exactly what they did, ladies and gentleman. Unfortunately for them, they were no better at faking up evidence than they were investigating crime. For one thing, they made up a suspiciously large number of drug transactions...10 in an hour is a *lot*...which was bound to draw attention. Even more suspicious was the fact that not even *one* buyer was arrested. The explanation they came up with---that Johnson did not have any officers in place to make these arrests----didn't help matters, because they couldn't explain why they didn't follow normal police procedure by arranging for these buyers to be arrested by back-up officers."

I pause to gather my thoughts and give the jurors a moment to consider my argument so far. Then I take a deep breath and continue. "But that *still* doesn't explain the time change on the paperwork, which was made in a way that could hardly be missed, by crossing out the original typed time with a marker and writing in a new one by hand. Why didn't they type the phony time on the reports in the first place, after they concocted the story about the buyers?"

I look over the jurors, as if expecting one of them to explain it to me, then say, "The only reason I can think of is that these officers are not exactly the brightest bulbs in the box, and they forgot that if they failed to allow some time for Johnson to make his imaginary observations, the whole thing would fall apart. By the time this occurred to them, the paperwork had already been completed. What they probably should have done at this point was tear up the 75-48 and 75-49, and start over again with new, blank forms But, either because they thought it would be too much work to type up another set of reports, or some other reason, they just did a quick fix, ran a marker over the actual time Johnson went out on the job, 8:05, and changed it by an hour."

I look over at the prosecutor. "I expect Ms. Tallow to tell you not to be distracted by this minor clerical error in the police reports, and will urge you to concentrate on the important stuff, like the oh-so-honest testimony of her officers. I am confident however, that you will not buy the prosecution's pig in a poke," I say, holding up the investigation report. I return my gaze to the jurors. "Why am I so sure?" I ask, then immediately supply the answer, "Because, if these time entries were really just unimportant, meaningless mistakes, why did Johnson and Ralston blow their stacks when I asked them about it? And why did the Commonwealth stipulate that Johnson didn't leave the police station until 8 o'clock, instead of putting him on the stand to defend his sworn testimony? Why? Because, if he did go back up there...," I gesture at the witness stand, "...he would have to answer some hard questions."

I now face the empty chair in the witness box and fire a question at it. "Officer Johnson, yesterday you told the jury that you watched Mr. Gibbs for an hour and saw him make ten narcotics sales, but that was a lie, wasn't it?"

I jump up on the witness stand, and sit, now pretending to be Johnson. "No, it's true," I protest. "I saw the defendants make those ten sales."

I step back down, snatch Exhibits D-3 and D-4 off the table, and wave them at the witness chair. "This page from the desk log shows that on the night February 27, 1997, you signed out on this job at 20:02. The time written next to your signature in the vehicle log was 20:03, just three minutes before the defendants were arrested." I thrust the two pages at where I estimate Johnson's face would be. "Look at them, Officer," I demand. "How could you have been observing anyone for an hour, when you had only left the precinct three minutes earlier?"

I return to the witness stand, and once again become Johnson. "I…uh…the log books are…wrong," I say unconvincingly. "I went out to the location at 19:00 hours, just like I said."

I go back down to resume interrogating the empty chair. "Those log entries are consistent with the times originally in your 48 and 49, that you left at just after 20:00, aren't they?" I demand.

I return to the witness chair, once again the beleaguered PO Johnson, and silently shake my head.

Returning to my cross-examining role, I ask, "Officer Johnson, the fact is that you *didn't* see ten narcotics transactions on that night, that you didn't see even one, and that when you testified yesterday that you did, you were lying, weren't you?"

Ending my little play, I turn to face the jury again. "It's not too difficult to understand why the prosecution didn't want Johnson testifying again, is it?" Several jurors nod in agreement.

"Now, as I have said, you can expect Ms. Tallow to tell you to ignore this time evidence, but what you *won't* hear from her is any explanation of how Johnson could make an hour's worth of observations in three minutes, because what explanation is there, other than the obvious one, that Johnson was lying? You should also be prepared for an old standby argument prosecutors use after the credibility of their police witnesses has been shredded, and they don't have anything else. It goes like this: Johnson testified under oath that he saw the defendant selling drugs, so if you find Mr. Gibbs not guilty, then poor, honest Officer Johnson will be charged with perjury for lying under oath, fired by the police department, and probably go to jail, and it would all be *your* fault, members of the jury. And would an experienced police officer like Johnson take such a chance for a conviction in a routine drug case? No, of course not. So, despite the fact that his testimony has been completely discredited and is unworthy of belief, the prosecutor will tell you that you must believe it anyway."

I shake my head. "This is nonsense, of course. First of all, I would challenge Ms. Tallow or anybody else to name *one* example of a cop being charged with perjury because the defendant he testified against was found not guilty. She can't, because there are no such cases. Second, a verdict of not guilty only means *one thing*: that the Commonwealth failed to prove the defendant guilty beyond a reasonable doubt, and that's *all* it means. It does not mean or imply anything about whether any or all of the witnesses for the prosecution lied under oath. If police officers could be charged with perjury under those circumstances, so could civilian witnesses, and I'll bet none of you have ever heard of that. In fact, if a defendant testified in his own defense, denying the charges, was found guilty, under this reasoning, *he* could be held for perjury, too, which would violate both the federal and state constitutions. So, after you reach your verdict of *not* guilty, you will be able to enjoy a clear conscience, because absolutely nothing is going to happen to either Johnson, Ralston, or any other police officer, and nobody will be charged with perjury, even if that's what they deserve."

I pause and again survey the jurors, trying to make eye contact with each one before wrapping up. "Ladies and gentlemen, when you were selected to serve on this jury, you swore under oath that you would find Mr. Gibbs guilty *only* if the Commonwealth's evidence proved it beyond a reasonable doubt, and if they did not, you would find him not guilty. I am not going to ask you to do anything but keep that promise, without fear, or favor, or any special pleading. Because if you hold the Commonwealth to that standard, after you have considered all the evidence in this case, you will only be able to reach one verdict: not guilty. Thank you."

I sit down. I *think* my closing has pretty much demolished the Commonwealth's case, but that doesn't mean the jury sees it that way. And there is always a chance that Carla Tallow will dazzle them with a closing statement worthy of Clarence Darrow, to miraculously snatch victory from defeat... although I don't think that's very likely.

So, I sit up straight and listen very carefully when she launches into her peroration. After the first 15 minutes or so, when I hear her trot out the "cops don't lie" line I had predicted, I relax. Carla is not what I would call a spellbinder orator, and I feel reassured that the verdict will be based on the evidence, not the persuasive skills of the attorneys.

After Carla finishes, the judge calls us back to his robing room behind the bench to tell us what charges (that is, the applicable law of the case) he plans to read to the jury. He asks if either Carla or I have any special requests for the charge. Neither of us can think of anything beyond the standard instructions, so he sends us back out to listen to ninety minutes of exquisitely boring legal definitions and instructions being read from the bench in a monotone. I start to doze off, and have to force myself to sit up straight and keep my eyes open. A glance over at the jury box reveals that the jurors are not only awake, which is surprising enough, but even appear to be listening to the judge's instruction, which I find positively remarkable.

Eventually, as all things good or ill must, the charge mercifully comes to an end, and the jury is led away to a quiet room for deliberations. The two substitute jurors are now superfluous, and they are dismissed by the judge, who thanks them for their service.

The judge asks Ms. Tallow and me to remain in or nearby the courtroom for two hours, until 5 o'clock (17:00 hours, cop time,) so we'll be available if the jury reaches a quick verdict. If they don't, he will send them home, then come back to continue to deliberate in the morning. Then he goes back to his robing room to wait.

Carla comes over to my table. "I realize you have to put on a show for the jury, Mr. Heller," she says. "But I know you don't really believe what you said about my witnesses in your closing."

I wonder if she heard the same testimony I did. "Now, why would you think that?" I ask.

"Because you've been around long enough to know better," she tells me earnestly. "Johnson and Ralston are both good, honest cops, 20-year veterans, who would *never* fabricate evidence the way you claimed."

Is she *kidding*? I wonder. One look at her face tells me that she is dead serious. Carla is clearly a card-carrying member of the PCDNWC (Police Can Do No Wrong Club) if not the president of the local chapter, so I see no point in arguing with her. As debating the virtues of these two paragons of law enforcement would plainly be a waste of time, I change the subject to complain about Judge Cheever's unwarranted meddling in the matter of the stipulation, which is something we can agree on. Then we return to our places to wait.

As it turns out, the jury didn't deliberate very long. They return with a verdict in less than an hour: Not Guilty. Even I was surprised at how little time it took; it generally takes twelve strangers longer than that to decide where to have lunch.

Epilogue: A year or so after the Gibbs trial, I was reminded of Carla Tallow's touching faith in the integrity of those model peace officers, Ralston and Johnson, when I read a newspaper story about the former. Ralston had been charged with homicide. He was accused of murdering his wife when he found out she was having an affair and, eventually, gave a full confession.

Before he confessed, Ralston tried to throw the homicide detectives off the scent, by giving the lead detective investigating the case a forged letter that incriminated his wife's lover. He displayed the same subtlety and attention to detail when he fabricated *this* evidence as he and Johnson had in the Gibbs case. He wrote the fake letter with his *left* hand, so the handwriting wouldn't be recognized, then signed it with the name of his wife's boyfriend. But he made one little mistake (as even the most brilliant criminal mastermind will do,) when he overlooked the fact that his left-handed script did not bear the slightest resemblance to the actual handwriting of the boyfriend. When this was pointed out to him, Ralston immediately broke down and confessed to the crime.

I have no doubt that this incident had no effect whatsoever on Ms. Tallow's touching faith in the universal integrity of Philadelphia's Finest.

Snapshot: Deal: No Deal

As noted above, in big cities in this country, the great majority of criminal cases are disposed by plea agreements, rather than trials. It's not difficult to understand why: the courts are overwhelmed. When I was working in the Brooklyn DA's office, I remember hearing a rumor that the Legal Aid Society (the New York Public Defender) was threatening to paralyze the court system by taking all their cases to trial, if they didn't start getting better plea offers for their clients. I don't know if the story was true, but it would have made an effective a threat.

The Court is not *supposed* to be involved in plea bargains. Except for a few unusual situations, plea deals should be left exclusively to the prosecutor, the defendant, and his lawyer: the court has no legitimate role in the process. However, the reality is that judges routinely interfere, pressuring one side or the other (usually the defense) to make a deal, so they can demonstrate how efficient they are by clearing their dockets.

During my first year as a prosecutor in Brooklyn, I was the assigned ADA in Judge Kropotkin's room in Criminal Court. Criminal Court is the lowest trial court in New York, where misdemeanor cases are sent to courtrooms (called "Parts" for some reason,) and assigned to prosecutors so new that the ink on their law licenses is still wet. Given the tremendous volume of cases (in the three years I worked in Brooklyn there were over 100,000 arrests every year, most of them felonies) it would have been impossible to prosecute more than a fraction of them. So, 90 percent of the felony charges were reduced to misdemeanors and sent, along with the DUIs, bar fights, simple possession of narcotics, and the other flotsam and jetsam, to the freshly-minted ADAs, like me. We each got a list of 150 or so cases, which we were expected to dispose of in any way we wanted, other than allowing them to be dismissed for failure to prosecute., This last part was a secret, known to only a handful of my fellow novice ADAs, the ones who went out drinking after work with their supervisors, a group that did not include me. If any of your cases were dismissed for failure to prosecute, that was a black mark against your name, and would delay your promotion in the office.

On the other hand, nobody cared how many ACDs (Accelerated Conditional Disposition) for which the penalty was six months unsupervised probation (meaning basically, no probation at all,) after which the charge was automatically dismissed. As a practical matter, an ACD was a dismissal by another name, but on the year-end statistics, it did not count as a dismissal, which was all that mattered to the DA.

Anyway, Judge Kropotkin made it clear that *he*--- not some wet-behind-the-ears whippersnapper of an ADA---was in charge of plea offers. On the other hand, I believed that, because the cases had been assigned to *me*, they were my responsibility and no-one else's. So, if I didn't agree with one of Kropotkin's proposed plea deals, I would say so.

The result was an ongoing series of skirmishes that more than once ended with the judge ordering my supervisor, a quivering mass of Jell-O named Bob, to come up to the courtroom, where Kropotkin would order him to order *me* to do as I was told. Matters came to a head one day, when Kropotkin decided what the offer on a misdemeanor assault would be. He generously characterized it as, "fair and reasonable."

"Maybe it is, Your Honor," I told him, "but it's not what we're offering."

With this, the judge hit the roof, ejected me from his courtroom, and told me never to return. Possibly he considered this a punishment. I was transferred to a different room, and some other lucky person took over the list in Kropotkin's room. I got along fine with my new judge, by the way.

Judicial interference of another kind produced the strangest guilty plea of my career. The facts are relatively straightforward, if not especially appetizing. My client was a young man with a wife and a toddler son. He was a laborer, performing hard, physical work for 10, sometimes 12 hours a day for minimum wages. Unlike most of my clients, he had no criminal record either as a juvenile or an adult, and had never even been arrested. That may not sound like anything special, if you are white, middle class, and grew up in the suburbs, but for somebody born and raised on the mean streets of the North Philadelphia ghetto, it was notable.

On the day of the incident, he returned home exhausted after 10 hours at work, where he immediately discovered that his wife was not having a good day. The moment he crossed the threshold, she snarled that their one-year-old son had been misbehaving, and she had been forced to punish him.

The punishment consisted of tying the boy to a hot radiator and leaving him there all day, ignoring his screams. My client looked at his son, who was by then asleep or unconscious, then at his wife. He knew she had a violent temper, and she looked ready to explode if he did or said anything that displeased her, so he decided to leave things as they were until he could calm her down. After a long, soothing talk, she did and he was able to put her to bed for the night. Only then, an hour after he had come home, did he return to the living room, release his son and call an ambulance. The radiator inflicted third degree burns on the boy's arms, neck and back. My client did not dispute the above facts.

The District Attorney charged the wife with Aggravated Assault, a Felony of the 2nd Degree, when the perpetrator intentionally causes serious bodily injury on another person, and Endangering of the Welfare of a Child, a Felony of the 3rd Degree. In general, a person cannot passively commit a crime, because most crimes require an intentional act. EWOC is one of the few exceptions to this rule, as, under certain circumstances, a person can be charged for *failure* to act.

Under our system of law, private citizens have no legal duty to help others, report crimes or suspicious behavior to the authorities, or cooperate with the police, even if they are eyewitnesses to a crime. To take an extreme example, if someone tells you he bought an assault rifle and is going to use it to shoot up the neighborhood elementary school, you could not be charged with a crime for failing to report him, even if the person showed you the weapon and ammunition and described his plans with you in detail. If he subsequently went out and massacred a dozen fifth graders, that *still* would not subject you to any criminal liability, because you don't have any general duty to protect other people. Criminal law, usually, does not impose a duty to act.

Endangering the Welfare of a Child (EWOC) is a special case, however. When someone is the custodian of a minor, a parent or someone acting in the place of a parent (Latin: *loco parentis*), such as a teacher or an institution like a school, then that person or institution has a positive duty to protect the minor from harm. Under those circumstances, even if the custodian doesn't actively harm the minor, he or she could still be guilty of EWOC, if he lets the child starve, for example, or doesn't seek medical attention if her charge fell sick.

So, I agreed with the charges of Aggravated Assault and Endangering the Welfare of a Child against the wife. She had committed the first offense by tying her son to a radiator, which she knew or should have known would cause serious injuries, and as his parent, had endangered the boy's welfare by the same act. Likewise, my client had committed EWOC, in his case by his failure to act, when he didn't untie the boy and get him to the hospital immediately, even if he was afraid of his wife (unless she was waving a gun around and was threatening to shoot him.)

But the District Attorney also charged my client with Aggravated Assault, a crime he had most definitely *not* committed. The crime of assault requires an intentional act or an act so reckless that it amounts to intent (for example: dropping bricks on cars from a highway overpass. You may not intend to hurt anyone in particular, but the action is so dangerous that it is almost certain to do so). While the husband was not a candidate for Father of the Year, neither was he responsible for his wife's criminal acts. He hadn't helped her when she assaulted the boy, had not even been present when she committed the crime, so he had neither committed the crime himself nor participated in it as an accomplice or as part of a conspiracy.

The ADA assigned to the case was the kind for whom prosecution is not just a job, but a Calling, and probably would have derived considerable satisfaction from prosecuting heretics for the Spanish Inquisition. Not one to let the law get in the way, she decided that my client was just as guilty as his wife, and therefore should be charged with the same offenses.

I will take a moment here to explain the nature and purpose of preliminary hearings, since they are not held in every jurisdiction, and therefore may be unfamiliar to some readers. In Pennsylvania, when someone is charged with a felony, before the case can be sent to the Court of Common Pleas for trial (or more likely, a plea,) a preliminary hearing is held before a district justice (commonly known elsewhere as "justice of the peace,") or in the City of Philadelphia, a judge of the Municipal Court. At the hearing, the Commonwealth must produce a *prima fascia* case (Latin: "at first appearance," or "at first face,") that is, present credible evidence in support of each element of the crime charged. This usually means that the absolute minimum evidence is presented, and often consists of hearsay that would not be admissible at trial as, for example, allowing the police to read statements supposedly taken from witnesses, instead of requiring live testimony. This is done primarily to prevent defense counsel from getting a chance to cross examine the witnesses before the trial. Since this hearing is only for the limited purpose stated above, the court doesn't take defense evidence into consideration when deciding whether to hold the case for trial. I had hoped the assault charge would be dismissed at the preliminary hearing, which was what should have happened, but I wasn't counting on it. Unfortunately, in this instance, the case was assigned to one of the worst judges in the Municipal Court, Senior Judge Harold Crabbe. As usual, Judge Crabbe didn't allow the facts or the law to confuse the issue, holding the case for trial without bothering to ask the Commonwealth how my client could commit an assault by doing nothing.

When I attempted to educate Judge Crabbe on the law by reading the statute from the Crimes Code, he cut me off and said, "The defendant is held for court on all charges, Mr. Heller. Would you like me to hold a hearing to review his bail, in light of his changed status?" In other words, he was threatening to raise my client's bail, which would land him in the county jail until trial if he couldn't make the new bail, if I didn't shut up. Since I wasn't about to risk that and he obviously wasn't going to listen anyway, I folded my tent and gave up.

In the calendar room, the first stop for a case in Common Pleas court [this is where cases are assigned to the courtrooms where they will eventually be tried or otherwise disposed of] I received the discovery packet and plea offer from the DA. My client was offered three years probation for Aggravated Assault and EWOC, exactly the same as his wife. Although he would be pleading guilty to a crime he hadn't committed, I reluctantly advised him to take the deal.

Why? Because the allegations, which we would have to concede were true, were not the kind that would make for a sympathetic jury. I thought it unlikely that a typical jury would be persuaded by legal arguments about the elements of assault, after hearing that he had left his infant son tied to a radiator, and being shown lots of grisly, close-up pictures of the third-degree burns. And, if he was found guilty of aggravated assault at trial, he was likely to get a prison sentence, instead of probation.

After I explained this to him, my client agreed to take the DA's deal, the case was given a new date, and two weeks later, the case was in front of Judge Marsha Geary for the plea. I didn't know much about her, so I didn't really know what to expect.

After a few preliminary questions, to make sure everyone was on the same page, the judge asked my client if he was voluntarily pleading guilty to Aggravated Assault and Endangering the Welfare of a Child. After he answered that he was, she turned to the Assistant District Attorney and said, "The Commonwealth will now state the factual allegations and charges to which the defendant is pleading guilty."

The ADA got through the EWOC charge well enough, but she ran into trouble when she began to recite her version of Section 2702(a) of the Criminal Code, Aggravated Assault, from the indictment.

"The defendant committed this crime, in that, on the above-captioned date, he did inflict serious bodily injury to…" [here she inserted the name of the child] "…intentionally, knowingly, or recklessly…" At this point, the ADA hesitated for a moment, before she continued, "…or by permitting another person to do so, under circum-…"

That was as far as she got before Judge Geary interrupted. "Excuse me, counselor, but I am looking at the statute, and I don't see that last part," she said.

"Ah, yes…, that is no, Your Honor," the ADA answered, obviously flustered. "That is from a case, Commonwealth v. Pruitt…"

"If you have a copy, hand it up, please," the judge cut in again. I thought she sounded a little impatient. "And give one to counsel as well, if you haven't already." [She hadn't.]

The prosecutor silently handed a photocopy of the three-page opinion to the clerk, who passed it up to the judge, and another to me. On the first page, I saw that this was not a decision of the Superior

Court or the Supreme Court, but from a Common Pleas Court in Cumberland County. So even if it was impeccably written and researched, I anticipated that it would have roughly the same precedential value in Philadelphia Common Pleas Court as an MBA from Trump University.

A quick examination of the opinion revealed that it cited not a single case in support of this novel interpretation of the assault statute, and read as if it had been written by a first-year law student. In my opinion, the paper the decision had been printed on would have been more usefully employed wrapping yesterday's fish.

The Judge must have reached a similar conclusion. After she finished reading the case, she pushed the pages to one side, and asked the prosecutor, "Do you have anything else, counselor?"

Obviously, she didn't, or she wouldn't have offered the judge that pathetic Cumberland County case, but I had to give her credit: just because she didn't have a leg to stand on didn't stop her. She tried to hop along on one leg. "If I may, Your Honor, the facts of that case..."

The judge did not allow the ADA to embarrass herself any further. She was silenced by the thud of the gavel announcing the court's verdict: "On the charge of Aggravated Assault, Section 2702 (a), I find the defendant not guilty."

I suppose it must have happened before, but I don't know of another case of a defendant pleading guilty being found not guilty.

Four: Pancakes and Syrup

In the course of my career, I have represented many unsavory characters, which is what you tend to get with criminals. More often than not, they were repeat offenders, because as it turns out, that's who commits most of the *serious* offenses (I do not include narcotics arrests, which stem from addiction, rather than a criminal lifestyle.) For most people, one trip through the gears of the justice machinery is enough. But not for the career criminal who, on the whole, is not very intelligent, rarely has the patience to plan his crimes in advance and is, for these reasons, likely to be arrested, even though, as we have seen, the average cop is no Sherlock Holmes.

I will share one case among many excellent choices to illustrate the above generalizations: Commonwealth v. Brandon Cooks. Cooks was a three- or possibly four-time loser, although he was not a candidate for the mandatory 10-year, 20-year or life sentences reserved for repeat offenders (aka "three-time losers,") as he had not been convicted of the specific crimes that trigger these punishments. This was certainly a matter of luck on his part, since Mr. Cooks was, in my considered judgement, only a little smarter than a bag of rocks.

I had been appointed at a very late stage in the case. For reasons unknown (to me, anyway,) Mr. Cooks and his attorney had suddenly parted company on the previous court date, when the case was scheduled to go for a bench trial (that is, a nonjury trial.) In any case, Cooks needed a new lawyer who would hit the ground running, and be ready to try the case on the next court date.

Enter yours truly. I had been given the discovery two weeks before the trial date, and found time to visit Mr. Cooks at CFCF (Carson-Fromhold Correctional Facility, where he was an involuntary guest of the county, due to both his inability to post $5000 cash bail and a detainer for a possible violation of probation from a previous conviction, the latter being this new arrest.

Mr. Cooks was not especially forthcoming when I saw him in the county lockup. When I reviewed the allegations on the police reports with him, he seemed sluggish and half-asleep. When I asked for his version of events, he mumbled something I couldn't make out, then fell silent. When I asked if he knew of any witnesses who might help his case, his response was much the same. Maybe he was going through withdrawal from something, I don't know.

My patience, never one of my notable traits, started to fray. "Tell me what you want me to do, Mr. Cooks," I said at last. "What's your pleasure? Do you want me to try the case, or do you want to take the plea offer? I'm your attorney, and I'll do whatever you want, but you have to choose one thing or the other."

This finally got his attention. He stared at me through the most bloodshot eyes I had ever seen. They looked like two baseballs of lean bacon. "What do *you* think I should do?" He mumbled.

"Well," I said, "given that you have no witnesses, no defense, and that you were caught practically in the act, I don't see much chance of winning at trial, so I think the only practical thing you can do is take the offer. It's not unreasonable." This was easy for *me* to say, since I wasn't going to be doing the time. Still, it was good advice. "It's 1-3 years upstate, and would be concurrent with whatever you get for the VOP [Violation of Probation.]"

Cooks considered the matter for a little while. "Can you get a better deal for me?" he asked hopefully.

"Considering we have nothing to bargain with, this is as good an offer as you're likely to get," I said. "If the DA really wanted to put the screws to you, he wouldn't make any offer. Then you would have the choice of pleading to the docket [pleading guilty to all charges] and leaving your sentence up to the judge, or go to trial. Either way, you would definitely get at least one-to-three upstate, and probably more."

He pondered this advice, then nodded. "Okay, then I'll take the deal."

"Smart move," I told him. "I'll see you in court."

A few days later, I was back at the Criminal Justice Factory before the Honorable Judge Llewellyn Gordon, in the matter of Commonwealth v. Cooks. While I was in the courtroom reviewing the details of the plea with the ADA, a court officer tapped me on the shoulder, and said, "They have your client upstairs, if you want to talk to him now before we bring him out." When prisoners are brought into the courthouse, they are kept in holding cells in the basement until their case is ready to be heard. Then they are taken up to the courtroom in a secure elevator, and placed in a cell adjoining the courtroom. If they are there for a jury trial, that's where they take off their prison jumpers and put on street clothes, so the jury won't know they are incarcerated.

In this case, there wasn't any jury, so Cooks was still wearing in his orange one-piece prison overalls. He was a great deal livelier than he had been when I had last seen him, at CFCF. In fact, he was downright agitated.

"What's going on?" he demanded. "Why'd they bring me down here for?"

"You're here to take a plea on the robbery case," I reminded him. "We talked about it when I saw you last week, remember?"

He squinted at me. "Plea? I don't know what you're talking about. I don't remember nothing about no plea," he said, growing more excited as he spoke. He pointed at me. "You're trying to sell me down the river, just like my last lawyer."

Huh, I thought. So, he doesn't want to take the plea, after all. That was okay with me. "I'm not selling you anywhere, Mr. Cooks," I assured him. "Nobody can make you plead guilty, if you don't want to. The prosecution witnesses are here, so we can try the case today, if that's what you want."

"Yeah, that's what I want, all right. I ain't taking no plea," he repeated.

"That is your right," I said. "Since we're going to try the case, let's just take a minute to review the facts again before we start."

There was a knock, and a court officer appeared, craning his neck around the door. "Mr. Heller, the judge wants to know if you're ready for that plea," he said.

I'm ready, I thought, but Mr. Cooks has other ideas. "You'll have to tell him there's been a slight change of plans. My client just informed me that he's no longer interested in the plea offer. We're going to trial instead."

"Then, you'd better come out and tell the judge and the DA yourself" he said.

"I'll be right out, as soon as I finish preparing the defense with Mr. Cooks," I said, wondering what defense that might be.

"All right, but make it quick, please," the court officer urged. "Everybody's waiting." He backed out, closing the door behind him.

"Now, Mr. Cooks," I said, returning my attention to him, "I need to go over the facts with you, again, so I can prepare the best possible defense, okay?"

"Yeah, okay," he answered.

I read aloud from the investigation: "The complaining witness, Mrs. Katherine Daugherty, told the police that at approximately 8AM on Monday, January 16 of last year, she was walking through the lower level of The Gallery..." [an underground shopping mall in Center City,] "...when an individual later identified as Brandon Cooks slammed into her from behind, knocking her to the ground and wrenching away her purse, which was on a strap over her left shoulder. She immediately cried for help. The Gallery was crowded, because it was rush hour, and the individual who had knocked her over only got a few feet before he was tackled by two civilians, who held him until the arrival of police officers. One of the men returned her purse, which now had a broken strap. Officers responded within a minute or two of the incident, took the suspect into custody, and asked Ms. Daugherty to identify the man who had knocked her down and taken the purse, which she did. The witness refused medical attention, and stated that she had not been injured."

I stopped, looked up at Mr. Cooks, and added, "They also have two eyewitnesses, who saw you steal her purse. So, it looks like they have a pretty strong case," I summarized, understating the situation considerably. "We don't have any witnesses except you, so your only chance is to testify in your own defense. So, tell me what happened, and why the Commonwealth witnesses are wrong." This should be interesting, I thought.

"I'm not guilty," he insisted. "I didn't do nothing to that lady."

"That's a good start," I said encouragingly. "But you need to be a little more specific. What happened, exactly?"

"I don't know," he said. "All I remember is one second I was walking around in The Gallery, and the next second, the cops are putting me in a police car."

"Ah?" I remarked, for lack of anything better.

"Listen man: I was so high on pancakes and syrup, I don't know *what* I did," he said. This did not mean that he had become intoxicated by consuming a short stack at the local IHOP. "Pancakes and syrup" was street jargon for Xanax washed down with codeine-based cough syrup.

"So, you can't really testify that you didn't rob Mrs. Daugherty, then," I said. "That doesn't help us much, I'm afraid."

"You *gotta* get me off, Mr. Heller," Cooks said. Once again, he protested his innocence, "I didn't do *nothing*."

Get him *off*? I thought as I went back out to the courtroom. He needed a miracle that would make the parting of the Red Sea look like a card trick to beat this case.

As soon as I appeared, the ADA and judge pounced on me. "Mr. Heller," Judge Gordon said, beckoning me to approach. "Would you kindly tell me what the *hell* is going on?"

Before I could answer, the prosecutor added, "Is he going to plead or not?"

I shook my head. "Not. He says, and I quote, 'I didn't do nothing,'" I told them, "So he's not going to plead to anything."

"For Chrissake, this is ridiculous!" the ADA blurted. "What's his defense?"

That was the question, all right. What possible argument could I make? Suddenly I was struck by an inspiration. "Well, he was high on pancakes and syrup at the time," I said, "so high that he didn't know what he was doing, and can't even remember what happened."

"So what?" the ADA demanded. "Intoxication is not a defense to robbery."

"True," I agreed. "But robbery is a crime of specific intent," I pointed out. This means that the Commonwealth must not only prove that the defendant took property from another person by force, but also that he did so *intentionally*. You can't commit a robbery by accident. "Mr. Cooks was so spaced out on drugs at the time, that he was unable to form the required intent for robbery...or any other crime, for that matter," I added.

I thought it was pretty good for something I had just made up on the spot. At least it was plausible enough to make the prosecutor hesitate. "That's not right...," he started, then stopped to consider exactly why it was wrong.

The judge now took a hand. "Even supposing you're right on the law, Mr. Heller...,"

I was already doing better than I expected, and happy to get even this hypothetical concession with my improvised defense.

"...What proof do you have of your client's mental state, other than his own testimony?" He finished.

None, of course, I thought. But I was having so much fun making bricks without straw, that I was in no hurry to give up. I thought about it for a second or two. "Well, the Commonwealth's witnesses may provide it. Maybe they thought he looked like he was not in his right mind at the time," I suggested.

The judge took a deep breath and let it out. "This has been an interesting discussion of legal theory," he said, "but it's over...*now*. Mr. Heller, I want you to go back and tell Mr. Cooks that *when*, not *if*, I find him guilty of F-3 Robbery after trial, he is *not* going to get 1 to 3, he is *not* going to get the guideline sentence of 24 to 48 months. What he *will* get is the statutory maximum: 5 to 10 years, and that sentence will run consecutive to his VOP time. Tell him that comes from the judge, will you?"

"I will, Your Honor," I promised, "and if he has even one working brain cell after doing all those pancakes and syrup, I think he'll take the plea."

I returned to the holding cell, and after an unnecessarily long debate, managed to convince Mr. Cooks that his best interests would be served by taking the plea offer. The plea went off in a routine fashion, somewhat to my surprise, as I half-expected the client to disrupt the proceedings.

Postscript: A year or two later, I was appointed to represent Mr. Cooks on another arrest, this one for selling heroin. The first time I saw him on the new case was in court, at a scheduling conference [this is one of the many, many wearisome procedural steps before a case gets listed for trial, that I had promised to spare you. I guess you can stand one little scheduling conference.] I had only been appointed a few days earlier, and as Cooks was serving time upstate, I had not yet had a chance to talk to him. Evidently, he had been thinking about the earlier case, because when he sat down at the table next to me, the first thing he said was, "Why did you sell me down the river on that robbery, Mr. Heller?"

Commentary: Judges-When the Refs Play for the Other Team

Judges are supposed to be arbiters, charged with impartially enforcing the rules of evidence to ensure a level playing field at the trial. Whatever their true feelings, like baseball umpires or referees at a football game, not only are they expected to both understand the applicable law and apply it fairly to both sides, but refrain from showing even the *appearance* of favoring one side over the other. They must instead at all times display Olympian detachment and complete indifference to the eventual outcome.

The foregoing is a description of the Platonic ideal of a trial judge, rather like a sub-atomic particle that should exist in theory, but hasn't been found in the real world. There's a good reason for this: judges are human beings, and thus by nature flawed and imperfect. This is not to say there are not judges who honestly strive to meet this these lofty standards, because there are. Unfortunately, this was not true of the judges in most of my cases.

My practice was geographically limited (Kings County, NY DA's office, Philadelphia, and a handful of cases in suburban Philadelphia counties), and my experiences may not be applicable to other jurisdictions. Possibly the courts of Illinois, Washington, and Alabama are presided over by veritable Solomons dispensing equal justice for all, without fear or favor (well, maybe not Alabama.) I can't say. But I do feel safe in stating that in the Philadelphia County Court of Common Pleas, a defendant's chances of having his case heard by a judge who does not actively favor the prosecution, is less than 50-50…a *lot* less.

Oddly enough, former criminal defense attorneys often end up having the most pro-prosecution bias after they have been elevated to the bench, as I was surprised to learn. I suppose the attitude of these former defense attorneys was a reflection of their experiences defending various dirtbags, skells, and mutts (to employ the colorful argot of the NYPD) for so many years, which probably made them cynical about human nature. What they forget, however, is that *sometimes* an innocent person was arrested, and in any case, all defendants, guilty or not, are entitled to a fair trial.

On the other hand, it is *not* true that all former prosecutors put their thumbs on the scale in favor of the Commonwealth. One of the very best judges in Philadelphia Common Pleas in my time, the Honorable Glen Bronson [real name], had been in his previous incarnation, the US Attorney for the Eastern District of Pennsylvania. Despite this background, when I appeared before him, I never had the slightest doubt that my client would get a fair trial in Judge Bronson's courtroom.

I know of no foolproof way to select judges, but I am all too conscious of how not to do it. In Pennsylvania, we use a time-tested system for producing biased, incompetent, and ignorant judges: elections.

This is a *very* bad thing. All one needs to become a judge in Pennsylvania is a law license, political connections and sufficient money to get a party endorsement to garner enough votes to win one of the open judgeships. That's it.

What's wrong with this? Plenty. The turnout for judicial elections is minimal; the bulk of the votes are cast by party regulars and whoever the ward leaders can round up in the neighborhoods. Nobody knows anything about the qualifications of the candidates, and probably are not aware of the generic ratings of "Recommended," "Highly Recommended," and "Not Recommended," issued by the Philadelphia Bar Association, which have considerably less effect on the outcome than the position of the candidate's name on the ballot (the closer to the top, the better the chances.)

For an example, I give you the Honorable Charles Wagner. Before taking the robes, Wagner had been a career politician in the state legislature. While he did have a law degree, his courtroom experience was, for all practical purposes, nil.

It was my good fortune to appear before the newly elevated jurist for his first trial. The ADA and I soon discovered that Judge Wagner had a truly profound lack of knowledge of the law; in particular, he was a veritable mountain of ignorance when it came to the simplest and most basic procedures of a jury trial. For example, he did not know how to summon a panel of selectmen (the potential jurors,) nor how the selection process worked, nor the difference between challenges for cause and peremptory challenges. And this barely begins to indicate the emptiness between His Honor's ears. It was not that he gave the impression that he had never presided over a jury trial before; rather it seemed as if he had never *seen* one before, even on television. I thought that anybody of normal intelligence who had seen a decent trial movie, *My Cousin Vinny*, for example, probably knew more about how a jury trial should go than Judge Wagner.

And yet, despite his near-total state of ignorance, Judge Wagner was not the least abashed by his appalling lack of knowledge. Almost from the beginning, he began threatening me with contempt charges for raising objections (which he invariably overruled,) asking questions he did not like on cross examination, generally interfering with the defense, and doing whatever he could to ensure that the defendant would not get a fair trial.

I was reminded of one of Rumpole's cases, where the presiding judge kept butting into Rumpole's cross.

"Your Honor," the great fictional barrister said at last, "the art of cross-examination is much like walking a tightrope."

"Oh, is it, Mr. Rumpole?" the judge asked.

"Yes," Rumpole answered. "One gets on so much better, when one is not *constantly interrupted.*"

That was exactly what I felt like saying to the arrogant, brainless Judge Wagner. I didn't, of course, because I had no desire to spend time in jail for contempt of court, nor could I afford the $1000 or $1500 fine that would likely result. But I did *think* about it.

Wagner was proud of his "tough on crime," sentencing, frequently expounding his theories of penology in newspaper and radio interviews. Apparently, his ideas failed to impress the Pennsylvania Supreme Court, which forced him to retire after 15 years on the bench, after a particularly egregious legal misdeed.

If you are wondering whether Wagner's retirement might have been voluntary, you need only look at the job he took after stepping down from the Court of Common Pleas. He became a Hearing Officer for the Parking Authority, and spent eight hours a day for two years listening to parking violation cases. I hope the service did not overtax his judicial skills.

Five: They Never Convict a Funny Man, Part One

One of my more memorable cases was Commonwealth v. Harris, in which a wrongful conviction was overturned and an innocent man set free, a case I will always remember as a Pyrrhic victory.

George Harris had been represented by an attorney from the Defenders Association by the name of Mack, and had been convicted of Aggravated Assault after a waiver trial (another term for "bench trial."). His conviction was appealed and reversed by the Pennsylvania Supreme Court, who granted him a new trial and ordered that a new attorney be appointed to represent him. This is where I entered the case.

Before I even met the client, I reviewed the discovery, the transcript of the original trial, and the Supreme Court opinion. His conviction had been overturned on the grounds of ineffective assistance of counsel, in other words, that his attorney had screwed up so badly that Harris had been denied a fair trial. This claim is often raised on appeal, but almost never granted.

Specifically, the ineffectiveness was the failure of defense counsel to obtain a psychiatric evaluation of his client before the trial. The Supreme Court found this to be a particularly egregious error in view of Harris's background: he had been given a medical discharge from the Navy for paranoid schizophrenia, and had been in and out of various mental health facilities ever since. At the time of his arrest, his sole income came from Social Security, who evaluated him as 100 percent disabled by mental illness. The court found that, in view of his history, it was more likely than not that if he had been examined by a psychiatrist, Mr. Harris would have been found unfit to stand trial.

I only had to read the first page of the trial transcript to decide that his attorney had been incompetent, but not for the same reason cited by the Supreme Court. I had to shake my head and wonder what could possibly have induced Harris's attorney to advise his client to allow his guilt or innocence to be left in the hands of Judge Rhinehart Mueller.

Judges with their thumbs on the judicial scales were hardly uncommon in Common Pleas, and they almost always favored the prosecution. By my estimate, they constituted a plurality of the jurists, if not an outright majority. But Judge Mueller was in a category of his own. Among the regulars at the Plant, prosecutors and defense alike, it was agreed that a waiver trial in front of Rinehart was equivalent to a slow guilty plea. That was why practically all the cases in his room were either guilty pleas or jury trials.

When I finally met the client, I immediately understood why he had been diagnosed with paranoid schizophrenia. When I asked him a question, he would begin speaking at a normal speed in a reasonably coherent manner. But he would quickly become excited, and start talking faster and faster, until his words all ran together in a way that was very difficult to understand. With some practice, I found that it was possible to make out what he was saying, but that wasn't much help, because he was unable to express himself in anything but an inscrutable jumble of apparently unrelated thought fragments. This is known in the psychiatric trade as a "flight of ideas."

After talking with him for a while, I began to get a fair idea of his story. He and his wife Lauren had been arguing off and on for several days, when he came home to find the front and back doors were locked, and she would not let him into the house. At first, she would not even speak to him, but eventually after he raised a sufficient commotion, she came over to the door, and without opening it, told him that she was kicking him out and he would have to go find another place to live.

Since the house had been purchased entirely with his money, and his wife had not contributed a cent, he considered the house least as much his property as hers, and was not prepared to follow her suggestion. Instead, he entered the house through the door to the cellar, then went up to try the door at the top of the basement stairs that opened onto the dining room. This door did not have a lock, but when he tried to push it open, he discovered that somebody on the other side was pushing back, trying to keep him out.

Although he was not a big man (he was approximately as tall as me, 5'7" and weighed around 160 pounds), George Harris was solidly built and strong for his size, so he was able to eventually force the door open and enter. He saw that his wife was not alone. Also in the dining room was a large woman he had never seen before. This was Mrs. Edna Lincoln, like Mrs. Harris, a congregant at the First Jubilee Blessed Church of the Living God, and it was she who had been holding the door against him.

He was understandably upset at being ordered to leave his own house without any warning. Ignoring the strange woman, he went to over to his wife and, as he admitted, may have raised his voice, when he asked her, "What's happening here?"

While he was waiting for his wife to say something, Mrs. Lincoln sidled silently up behind him and shouted, "Jesus! Jesus! Jesus!" in his ear.

This startled him, and he spun suddenly to see who had bellowed in his ear, accidentally bumping into Mrs. Lincoln. The latter lost her balance, staggered back, and landed heavily on the dining room table. She was a substantial woman, and she proved to be more than the table could handle. It collapsed, throwing her to the ground, and causing her to sustain what Judge Mueller believed were serious bodily injuries.

Naturally, this was only *his* version; Mrs. Lincoln and Mrs. Harris told a rather different story in their testimony at the first trial, one which I expected them to repeat for the jury.

But before that, I had another duty, one that had been imposed on me by the Supreme Court: I had to have George Harris evaluated by a psychiatrist to determine if he was competent to stand trial. The bar for competency is an easy one to clear. It requires only that (1) the defendant understand the nature of the charges against him, and (2) that he is able to assist in his own defense. Despite his mental condition, I had no doubt that George Harris met these requirements, but it was plain that the justices of the highest court in Pennsylvania did not agree.

Neither, as it turned out, did George Harris. He had a distinct aversion to the entire tribe of psychiatrists. He did not tell me the reason, but I guessed that it was related to the number of times they had ordered him to be confined in mental hospitals, which provided no treatment and were overcrowded hellholes with living conditions that were at best, only marginally superior to those in state prison. I sympathized with his position, but there really wasn't any way to avoid it. I was finally forced to ask the judge to threaten him with a contempt of court charge before he would agree to give the court psychiatrist an interview.

Dr. Brian O'Neill, the court psychiatrist, should have had his license to practice medicine revoked for malpractice. He said Harris's thought processes were "logical and goal directed," and his affect was "appropriate and full range," a description which nobody who spent five minutes talking to him would recognize. When Harris said that he heard voices in his head, O'Neill suggested that he was lying, because he could not "specifically describe the voices." I particularly disliked the way the doctor disposed of another obvious symptom of severe mental illness, not with a psychiatric analysis, but a linguistic one: "He reported that he did not feel hopeless, but did feel helpless."

O'Neill did his best to minimize Harris's long psychiatric history. For example, the report said that he "underwent [sic] a medical discharge from the Navy," without mentioning that the medical condition in question was schizophrenia. Likewise, the fact that Harris was considered to be 100 percent disabled by both the Veterans Administration and Social Security was mentioned, but left out the disabling condition: paranoid schizophrenia. Harris's medical history escaped any mention in O'Neill's report to the court.

Instead, he came to the remarkable conclusion that, despite Harris' long history of mental illness, the diagnosis of schizophrenia by other doctors, his numerous involuntary commitments to institutions, the finding of his 100 percent disability by two federal agencies, and all the rest, that the man who had been able to fool so many doctors for so many years had at last been exposed by the brilliance of Dr. Brian O'Neill. Before he stated his opinion that George Harris was competent to face trial (surprise!) he added a gratuitous and quite irrelevant slander: "It is my opinion that Mr. Harris is embellishing his psychiatric symptoms for the purpose of avoiding prosecution [and is] a malingerer."

This mental health evaluation was such a piece of crap that, despite the fact that I also believed my client was competent to stand trial, I wanted to expose the unabashed quack who had written it, and rip him a new orifice. Expert witnesses are not excused from cross-examination any more than ordinary witnesses are. I made a motion asking that O'Neill be compelled to appear in court to testify under oath about his mental health evaluation, arguing that under the Sixth Amendment, a criminal defendant has the absolute right to confront and cross-examine witnesses against him, and that his report was hearsay and inadmissible.

I was not surprised when Mueller denied the motion on the most specious grounds. "The Sixth Amendment only applies to witnesses against a defendant," he said. "Dr. O'Neill is not a witness for or against anyone, but a neutral expert who, like the Court, cannot show favor to either side, and so, does not fall under the confrontation clause of the Sixth Amendment." I had to give him credit managed to say this with a straight face.

Having put me in my place, the judge went on, "Now that we've gotten that out of the way, let's get on with this trial."

The jury was empaneled at lightning speed, largely because Judge Mueller wouldn't let either ADA Jan McAfee or me ask the prospective jurors more than one or two questions on *voir dire*. The judge was a great believer in efficiency: he thought that every minute not directly spent on securing the conviction of a defendant was wasted. Fortunately for my client, despite Judge Mueller's efforts we somehow ended up with what I thought was a reasonable jury.

After a short opening statement by Jan and an even shorter one by me, we heard from the first, and as it turned out, only Commonwealth witness. Mrs.

Harris, who had testified for the prosecution at the first trial, didn't show up this time, which meant that Edna Lincoln and her medical records was the prosecution's whole case.

I knew that Edna Lincoln was a big woman, but I did not know how big, until she rolled into court overflowing her self-propelled wheelchair. She wasn't just *big*, she was immense, colossal, a veritable continent of flesh. She was so big that she could not get to the witness stand, because she was too wide to fit through the gate in the railing that separated the public area of the courtroom from the portion used to conduct court business, such as trials. So, her testimony was given from the other side of the gate, which was as far as she could get into the court. I am not dwelling on Mrs. Lincoln's obesity out of cruelty; it turned out to be very important in the outcome of the trial.

Edna Lincoln's testimony on direct examination was pretty consistent with her testimony at the first trial, and didn't contain any real surprises. In response to Ms. McAfee's questions, the witness explained that she had come over to the Harris residence to help Lauren Harris clean the house.

Her description of George Harris's arrival and what happened afterwards went like this:

ADA: When did you first see George Harris that night?

Witness: When he came up from the basement and pushed the door open.

ADA: What were you doing when he was pushing the door open?

Witness: Pushing back, trying to keep him out.

ADA: Why were you trying to keep him out?

Witness: Because Lauren didn't want him...

Before the jury could hear her say that Harris's wife didn't want him in the house, I cut in: "Objection. Calls for a hearsay response."

"Sustained," said Judge Mueller, to my mild surprise (it was mild because he had sustained a similar objection by Harris' counsel at the first trial.)

Ms. McAfee seemed to take this setback in stride, and picked up her direct examination where she had left off.

ADA: Now, what happened after he pushed his way in?

Witness: He ran right by me into the living room where Lauren was, and said to her, "What do I have to do, kill you?"

This was also hearsay, but I didn't object because it was admissible under one of the many exceptions to the hearsay rule, in this case, Rule of Evidence 805.1 Statement by a Party Opponent.

Now Ms. McAfee was ready to ask Mrs. Lincoln to describe the actual assault.

ADA: What did Mr. Harris do then?

Witness: He saw me, turned around and walked me back towards the dining room, then threw me from the living room into the middle of the dining room table. Then he ran in and threw me on the floor. Then he left the room. I didn't see where he went.

ADA: What did you do after he threw you on the floor?

Witness: Nothing. I couldn't move my arms or legs, couldn't move anything.

She went on to tell the jury how she was later taken to Einstein Hospital in an ambulance, and that she had been confined to a wheelchair ever since that day. (Ms. McAfee later introduced Mrs. Lincoln's medical records into evidence. They showed that she had suffered a spinal injury from the fall that made it impossible for her to walk.)

I thought this would conclude the witness' testimony, but Ms. McAfee tried to sneak in some new incriminating testimony that hadn't been introduced at the first trial.

ADA: Mrs. Lincoln, when you were in the hospital, did you learn that he had done something to your house?

I was on my feet shouting my objection before the ADA had finished her question. But the witness started to answer anyway. "I found out George Harris had gone..."

The Judge now stepped in. "There is an objection by Mr. Heller," he told her. "Don't say anything else until I have ruled."

This judge's words had no greater effect on Mrs. Lincoln than my objection had. She turned back to look at Ms. McAfee and continued "...that George Harris had broken the windows..."

I objected again, even more loudly than before. Ms. McAfee shook her head, and began explaining to the witness that she should shut up, "No, Mrs. Lincoln, you can't..."

Judge Mueller plainly did not like the way Mrs. Lincoln had blithely ignored his instructions. He flushed, leaned over in a threatening manner, and speaking slowly and with obvious sincerity, said, "If you say anything else before I have ruled on the defense objection, I will hold you in contempt." He paused to let her think about that, then asked, "Is *that* understood?"

This had the intended effect on Mrs. Lincoln. She looked wide-eyed up at the judge and nodded silently to indicate her understanding.

Now he summoned Ms. McAfee and me to approach. "Is the witness going to say that she personally saw the defendant do something?" He asked.

"Break the windows of her house," she explained. "No, Your Honor, she was in the hospital at the time, so it would have been impossible for her to see it. She was told that the defendant did it by someone who saw him."

"Your Honor," I said, "even if this wasn't hearsay, it's inadmissible on relevancy grounds. What does broken windows have to do with this alleged aggravated assault?" I answered my own question. "Nothing."

If Ms. McAfee had anything helpful to add, she didn't get a chance to say it. The judge said, "All right, I've heard enough argument. I'm ready to rule on the objection. Step back."

We returned to our respective counsel tables to hear, "The objection is sustained." This wasn't any kind of surprise. Even if Mrs. Lincoln hadn't pissed Mueller off, as a matter of law it wasn't a close call.

"Do you have any further questions for this witness?" the judge asked Ms. McAfee.

"No, Your Honor, I'm done," she said, settling into her seat. "Your witness, Mr. Heller."

I certainly hope so, I thought.

114

Snapshot: What Cops *Really* See

You will recall me complaining in the Time Cops chapter about canned police testimony in drug cases: "I've heard this same prefabricated evidence almost word-for-word a hundred times before...," and so on. When police testify about observations of narcotics sales, they always have a clear view of the suspect, and they can see every detail of the drug transactions, whether it happens in broad daylight or at 2 AM, rain or shine. Typically, drug dealers seem to go out of their way to make sure that the police can see their illegal activities. The cop will almost invariably testify that they saw the drug dealer hold out a small plastic packet or glass vial to the buyer, pinched between his thumb and forefinger, and that he received U.S. currency in return, which was also held out at arm's length, held between the buyer's fingertips.

I had one case where the arresting officer claimed that he saw the defendant take drugs from the trunk of his car, when the officer was observing from his three cars up, parked on the same side of the street as the defendant. Since the lid of the defendant's trunk would by necessity have been raised for him to have access to the trunk, I was unable to understand how the officer could have seen the defendant's actions through a solid metal trunk lid. So, I asked what seemed to me to be a natural question, "Did you use around-the-corner binoculars to see what my client was doing?" For some reason, this provoked an objection from the prosecutor that the judge sustained, so I never did find out how he saw around or through the obstruction.

As I did in the Time Cops trial, I would always ask narcotics cops if they had made video recordings of their observations, knowing that the answer would always be that the Philadelphia Police Department did not make videos, even when the cops in question were watching safely from a hidden location. As might be expected, when asked why not, the witness would explain that it was department policy made up above their pay grade, and they didn't know. I had long suspected the true reason for this policy, but it was not until I was appointed to represent James Vincent in a big joint city/state narcotics operation that those suspicions were confirmed.

At least 25 co-defendants and their counsel were gathered in the auditorium-courtroom, a room whose existence I had previously been unaware of, in the Philadelphia Criminal Justice Factory, along with representatives of the Philadelphia District Attorney, the Pennsylvania Attorney General, and a miscellaneous assortment of state and city cops from various units. We were all there for a preliminary hearing on charges of Possession with Intent to Deliver Controlled Substances, Sale of Controlled Substances, and Conspiracy to commit the foregoing offenses. Not only was this the biggest drug bust I had ever been associated with, but it was also by far the most lavish production of its kind I had ever heard of. The Joint Drug Task Force that mounted this operation had accomplished something that the Philadelphia Police Department had long ago determined was impossible, overcoming the seemingly insuperable difficulties presented by the operation of video equipment to record drug sales, so that we could now see exactly what the police saw!

A big screen had been set up on a raised platform in the front of the room, giving all present an unobstructed view of the proceedings. This, as it turned out, was considerably more than could be said for whoever was making the recordings.

The film showed a block of North Philadelphia at night. Everything had a greenish tint; a consequence of the infra-red night-vision photography. The object of the investigation was a house at the end of a block, at the corner of Sixth and Indiana in the section of the city known as the "Badlands."

The camera was focused on the porch of the house where, we were assured by police witnesses, the defendants were making narcotics sales. Oddly enough, the video did not show anyone holding out little packets at arm's length, nor anyone accepting said packets, nor anyone transferring U.S. currency to anybody else. We did not see anyone going to a stash on the curb, under the steps, to the trunk of a car, or anywhere else to retrieve small objects, as police invariably claimed they did before they started making arrests.

What we *did* see was this: a large number of people, anywhere from 35 to 50, milling around, walking up and down the block, and sometimes going up on the porch of the suspect house. On the porch could be seen a varying number of individuals doing indefinable things, but from the images on the screen, there was no way of knowing what those things might be.

They *might* have been buying and selling drugs, but they could just as easily have been discussing the prospects for the Eagles in the coming NFL season, comparing the merits of natural versus synthetic motor oils, planning exhibits for the upcoming Philadelphia Flower Show, or practically anything else. It was impossible to say.

So, this was what cops really saw during their observation sales cases. No little plastic vials, no folded U.S. currency, no transfers from one person to another. This video should have been made mandatory viewing for all observation drug cases in Philadelphia, probably in the entire country. It showed up narcotics cops for the liars they were, and revealed what a travesty these arrests really were.

As it happened, the Joint Task Force wisely did not rely on their singularly uninformative video tapes to make their cases. They also employed undercover cops to buy narcotics from the location, and these buyers identified the drug dealers and their assistants, including my client, based on close-up, personal observations. Of course, they may also have been lying, but that would be a lot more difficult to show. In the end, my client pled guilty to Possession with Intent to Deliver on this case and another open case, in return for a relatively mild sentence of 1½ to 3 years incarceration.

Six: They Never Convict a Funny Man, Part Two

This was the first time I had ever been involved in a re-trial of a case, and it offered some distinct advantages for the defense. I had a pretty good idea of what the main Commonwealth witness (and as it turned out, only witness,) was going to say, because I had a transcript of the first trial. In civil practice, it is commonplace for the attorneys on both sides to take sworn testimony from witnesses in pre-trial depositions. In criminal cases, the defense generally goes into a trial with police reports summarizing the statements of some witnesses, and a transcript from the preliminary hearing, which as noted earlier, is usually only a little better than nothing.

But this time, I had a written record of every word of the witnesses' testimony from the first trial, which gave me a much better than usual chance to prepare. And if the witness floundered during cross and tried to improvise new answers, it would be a simple matter to bring her back in line by confronting her with her own words from the first trial.

You have to be careful about how you cross-examine a witness like Mrs. Lincoln. You don't want to come off as bullying a wheelchair-bound, churchgoing senior citizen, especially if your client is alleged to have attacked her and caused terrible injuries. So, I began as agreeably as I could.

Me: Good afternoon, Mrs. Lincoln. I'm Mr. Heller, the defendant's attorney, and I'd like to ask you a few questions. Would that be all right?

Witness: Good afternoon, sir. Yes, that would be all right.

Me: Thank you. Now, I want to ask you about something you said in response to Ms. McAfee. You said that Mr. Harris came up from the basement of the house and forced open the door, is that right?

Witness: Yes, that's right.

Me: And that was the door between the basement stairs and the dining room, right?

Witness: Yes, sir.

Me: So, you were in the dining room when Mr. Harris pushed the door open.

Witness: Yes, I was trying to keep him out, because Lauren said ...

Me: Mrs. Lincoln, please just answer my question, and don't volunteer anything I didn't ask you about, all right?

(Witness nods.)

Me: Let me repeat the question. What room were you in when Mr. Harris came through the door?

Witness: The dining room.

Me: And you said that when he entered the dining room, Mr. Harris didn't pay any attention to you, but went straight into the living room where his wife was, isn't that right?

Witness: Yes.

Me: And he appeared to be very excited when he was talking to her, didn't he?

Witness: Yes. He was yelling and acting strange.

Me: And while he was yelling at Lauren in the living room, where were you?

Witness: Right where I was when he came in.

Me: Still in the dining room? You never left that room?

Witness: No, not that I remember.

Me: You said he noticed you at some point, correct?

Witness: Yes.

Me: And when he noticed you, you were in the dining room, weren't you?

Witness: I don't remember that.

Me: Well, you said he forcibly took you back to the dining room, so that means you must have come *out* of the dining room, doesn't it?

Witness: I'm not sure.

Me: This is the official transcript of the first trial. This is what it says... page 14, line 9, Ms. McAfee...Question (from Ms. McAfee): What is the next thing that the defendant does? Answer, by you: He saw me, grabbed me and walked me back to the dining room. Do you now recall saying that both at the first trial and here today, Mrs. Lincoln?

Witness: Yes, I suppose I did.

Me: You went into the living room, where the defendant was arguing with his wife, and you came up behind Mr. Harris and said something to him, because you wanted to get him away from Lauren, isn't that right?

Witness: Yes. He was acting very wild, and I was afraid he might do something.

Me: So, you came up behind Mr. Harris, and you said something to him, didn't you?

Witness: Yes.

Me: And you were excited yourself, so when you spoke to Mr. Harris, you shouted, didn't you?

Witness: I was excited, scared, so I might have raised my voice.

Me: In fact, you came up behind him and shouted, "Jesus, Jesus, Jesus," at the top of your lungs, directly in his ear, didn't you?

Witness: I don't remember what I said.

I was pretty happy with the first part of the cross-examination, which corroborated my client's version. Not only did she admit that she had come up behind him while he was talking to his wife, but she also said that she had shouted at him. If she had denied speaking to Mr. Harris, I would've been stuck with that answer, because I had no proof that she had, other than what he had told me.

Now, I was ready to go after the big prize. This was something that seemed like the most obvious point in favor of the defense, but was for some inexplicable reason, not pursued at the first trial.

Me: How far did you go into the living room, when you left the dining room to approach Mr. Harris?

Witness: Not far, only a little ways.

Me: Could you point to something in the courtroom to show the jury how far it was?

Witness: Maybe like about where you are standing.

Me: For the record, approximately four feet from the witness. So stipulated, Ms. McAfee?

McAfee: No objection.

Me: So, you were just outside the dining room when you came up behind Mr. Harris, correct?

Witness: Yes.

Me: Then, you say, he turned around, grabbed you and walked you back to the dining room, then picked you up and threw you across the room to land on the table. Is that right?

Witness: Yes, sir, that's what he did.

Me: You say he threw you. Do you mean that your feet left the ground, and you flew through the air to the table?

Witness: Yes. He picked me up and threw me like a bag of laundry, and I landed on my back on the table.

Me: Mrs. Lincoln, did you weigh about the same then as you do now?

Witness: Yes.

Me: And how much do you weigh?

Witness: Well, I'm not sure of the exact number…

Me: We don't need an exact number. Just tell us approximately, within 10 pounds either way, if you can.

Witness: I think I was about 360 the last time I was on a scale.

"Thank you, Mrs. Lincoln," I said. I went back to my seat, and announced "No more questions." I didn't need to ask her anything else. I had just created a reasonable doubt.

Snapshot: An Entertaining Video

When I was working for the Kings County DA, the office had a policy of video-taping DWI (Driving While Intoxicated) suspects who agreed to take the field sobriety tests. The tape was then put in the file given to whichever assistant was assigned the case.

For those of you who have never been stopped for drunk driving and have been denied the privilege of watching a driver being put through these tests, I will describe the tests used at that time. (I understand they use slightly different tests now.)

The first was the finger-to-nose test. The suspect would be told to extend his arms out to the sides, close his eyes, and touch the tip of his nose with his hands, alternating left and right. Then they walk heel-and-toe along a painted line, then turn and come back the same way. After that was the one-leg stand. The last and most difficult test is to bend over, pick up 3 twenty-five cent pieces from the floor, without losing your balance. This last test is not that easy even cold sober, particularly if, like me, you have put on some weight and are no longer in fighting trim.

The first thing I looked at in a DWI file was the BAC (Blood Alcohol Level) recorded by the Breathalyzer. A BAC of .10 % or higher while operating a motor vehicle was all the proof needed for a Driving While Intoxicated conviction. It did not matter if the driver looked and sounded perfectly sober, nor if he was in control of his car when he was stopped, nor if he passed the field sobriety tests with flying colors. A BAC between .10 and .07 % was a lesser offense, Driving While Impaired, the main difference being that the DUI entailed a mandatory six-month suspension of the driver's license. Anything below .07 was legal.

The BAC for this particular defendant was the highest I had ever seen or heard of: .35%, more than three times the legal limit. I was surprised that the fellow had even been able to put the key into the ignition, let alone operate it on the street. I popped the field sobriety test into the VCR, and sat back, expecting to see the defendant swaying like a tree in the wind, or staggering around in circles. I was in for a surprise.

The state trooper who made the arrest appeared on camera, stated his name, then the defendant's name, then explained that he would ask the suspect to take a series of field sobriety tests, that these tests were entirely voluntary, and he did not have to take them. Then the trooper asked the suspect if he understood and if he wished to take the tests.

The camera swung around to show the defendant. He was a dark-haired, swarthy, 36-year-old man, who appeared to be in unusually good spirits for someone who had just been arrested.

He grinned and said happily, "Yeah, sure, I'll take the tests. Why not?" He pointed at the camera, and asked, "Hey, am I gonna be on TV?" Without waiting for an answer, he waved at the camera, and asked, "Is it okay to say 'Hi' to my buddies?" Then, he shouted, "Johnny, hey, Johnny Carpelli, how you doin'…"

The trooper stepped in and explained that the camera was making a recording for law enforcement personnel, and that it would not be broadcast or shown to the general public.

If the suspect was disappointed, he disguised it well. "That cool, that's good," he said, nodding enthusiastically. "So, what do you want me to do?"

The stone-faced state trooper took him through the tests, one-by-one, and the suspect performed them all flawlessly. After the finger-to-nose test, the suspect turned to the camera and asked, "Did you get that?" After the heel-and-toe test, he asked the trooper, "How was that?" After the one-leg stand, he said, "Perfect, wasn't it?"

The climax of this show came after he had smoothly picked up the first two quarters and handed them back to the cop. When he got the third one, instead of putting it in the trooper's outstretched hand, he faced the camera and said, "Watch this!"

He flipped the quarter up over his head. Then he brought his hand out from behind his back, displaying the quarter he had just caught.

"You see that?" he demanded. He danced around as if he had just hit a walk-off home run in the 7th game of the World Series, shouting "Yes!" and trying to high-five the state trooper.

I took the tape to my supervisor, and played the tape for him. He broke out laughing when he saw the defendant's victory celebration, then sat back grinning after the tape ended.

"What a character," he said. He snorted one more time, then said, "I think you'd better offer him Impaired."

"Impaired?" I asked. "He blew a *.35*. He was so drunk we could charge him with *three* DWI's."

He shook his head. "Sure, it looks like a layup... to us. But suppose he takes a jury trial, which he will, unless his lawyer has the brains of a turnip. How are you going to convince a jury of ordinary citizens that he had three times the legal limit of alcohol in his system, but he could still catch a quarter behind his back? What do you suppose they'll think?"

I considered it. "They'll probably think the Breathalyzer blew a fuse," I said.

"Right," he agreed. "It doesn't matter how accurate the cops will say it was, even if they had calibrated it five minutes before he was tested."

"Actually, they might be right not to trust that test, now that I think about it," I said, now swinging around to the other extreme. "Maybe we shouldn't, either. How could he do that coin trick if he really was that drunk?"

"I bet he's one of those real serious drinkers, who probably has a .15 BAC when gets out of bed in the morning," he explained. "I've met a few like that. If either of *us* drank as much as that guy, we'd be out cold on the floor. But for him, it's just his normal condition. He probably wins a lot of money taking bets on that coin flip trick. Hell, he can probably catch it in one hand while he's guzzling vodka with the other. Give him an Impaired, and forget about it."

I got up, punched out the tape from the player, and started to put it back in the manila folder holding my file. My boss caught it on the way and said, "Just leave it with me, if you don't mind. I want to show it to some other people in the office. They'll get a kick out of it."

It wouldn't surprise me if he took that tape with him when he left the DA's office a few weeks later. At least, I never got it back. Which is a shame: I'm sure it would have been a *sensation* on social media.

Seven: They Never Convict a Funny Man, Part Three

After the cross-examination of Edna Lincoln, I thought the trial was going so well that I considered not calling Mr. Harris or putting on any evidence, and going right to closing argument, because I wasn't sure we needed to do anything else. In the end, however, I decided to go ahead with the original plan and put him on the stand. Why?

For one thing, the client had told me in no uncertain terms that he wanted to testify, and I doubted I could talk him out of it, even if I thought it was a bad idea, which I didn't. Anyway, Mrs. Lincoln had corroborated the most important parts of his story already, and would make his testimony even more effective.

At this point, you may be wondering where I got the name of this case; nothing particularly funny has happened so far. I thought the explanation should wait for the right moment in the trial, and this is it.

George Harris had a strange effect on his listeners. People would start to giggle when they heard one of his mixed verbal salads delivered at the speed of a professional auctioneer. I don't exactly know why other people found him so hilarious; he didn't have that effect on me. Possibly it was his earnest, ultra-serious manner when he spouted his usual jumble of words and thought fragments, like Professor Erwin Corey (some of you are old enough to remember this comedian's stand-up schtick. The rest of you can find him on YouTube.)

Here's a sample of his testimony below. I warn you that it probably won't seem that funny when you read it. In comedy, everything depends on the timing and delivery.

Me: What happened when you went home that day?

Witness: I lived there with my wife that afternoon and they took my clothes over my mother's house... my cousin's house prior to that. Mrs. Lincoln came in my house and started hollering and all this kind of stuff, and my wife was trying to get my Social Security and Navy disability, so what did they have to go and lock me out for?

(I can see some of the jurors trying to hide smiles.)

Me: Did you leave the house at some point?

Witness: I left at around 3 o'clock, and when I came back the light was on, but when I tried the door, it was locked because my wife and I had breakups so I knocked and she came to the door told me I had to move out, but why was Mrs. Lincoln there telling her what to do, when it wasn't none of her business about my pension.

(Several jurors have clapped their hands over their mouths and have turned away, so I won't be able to see them laughing. I wait a few moments for them to recover.)

Judge Mueller looks down disapprovingly at the jury, then growls, "Let's not waste any more time, Mr. Heller. If you have more questions for this witness, ask them."

What a grouch, I think. He's mad at the jury for laughing and not taking the case seriously enough, so who does he blame? The attorney, who's just doing his job. Typical.

"Certainly, Your Honor," I say. Mr. Harris and I are working together like a well-oiled machine. All I need to do is ask a question (the subject of the question hardly matters) and his answer has the audience...err..., I mean, the *jury* in stitches. With growing confidence, I resume the direct examination.

Me: Now, what happened after your wife came to the door and told you had to move out?

Witness: I knew I was living there, and I didn't lock the cellar, so I came in, up the stairs, and pushed the door open, went past this strange lady and saw my wife. So, I went over there and said 'What's happenin', and when I was talking to my wife, Mrs. Lincoln came up behind me and shouted in the back of my neck, and I didn't know who it was because me and my wife would have been together two years and never has no-one ever stayed there before, so I...

Court reporter: Could you slow down a little please?

(The entire jury has by now been infected, and several of them are red-faced from the effort of controlling their laughter. I see that Ms. McAfee is not immune to Mr. Harris's magic, either. She has a fist pressed against her lips, but I can see the corners of her lips curling up.)

Me: Mr. Harris, please try to speak a little more slowly, so the court reporter can take down your words, all right?

Witness: Yes, I'm sorry. I'll try.

Me: Now, you said Mrs. Lincoln shouted something at you from behind. Do you remember what she said?

I thought McAfee might object at this point on the grounds of hearsay, but she didn't, possibly because she was concentrating so much on not laughing that it slipped by her. *

Witness: She said, "Jesus, Jesus, Jesus!" real loud, just like that, it scared me, she lied and testified at the 25th District that she was in my house before, and that was a lie, she didn't even know my name, so how could she tell my wife to lock me out so she could get my pension?

The judge turns his chair to face away from the witness, but not before I see him clap his hand over his mouth. We've even managed to crack up Old Sourpuss! I believe we have done enough, and decide it's time for George and me to wrap up the act before we lose the audience.

Me: What did you do when she shouted in your ear?

Witness: I turned around real fast, and I was like, "What's the matter with you?" 'cause she snuck up on me like that and I bumped into her, and she telling you that I did the worst of the doing in touching her, if I was going to hurt her, not walked away and didn't come back and throw her over the table.

Me: So, are you saying that you accidentally bumped into Mrs. Lincoln, and she lost her balance?

Ms. McAfee: Objection. Leading.

Judge: It is, but I think I will allow Mr. Heller some latitude to direct this witness, in the interest of clarity. Overruled.

A miracle! I was momentarily stunned. Then, conscious that the spell of favorable judicial weather was unlikely to last much longer, I tried another leading question.

Me: And what happened to Mrs. Lincoln after you bumped into her, and she lost her balance?

Witness: She went backwards and fell on the dining room table, she fell on her neck, we had a chair that was on the side, my wife hasn't worked in seven months because she was having the baby, and when she was making dinner the night before I moved the chair back and there was a mouse under the chair, and I went and got the mouse out, I moved the chair, and Mrs. Lincoln knew my house, so when she jumped back from me she speculated that there would be a chair there, but by me founding a mouse on Thursday I moved the chair.

This was an excellent explanation that doubtless cleared up everything for the jury, several of whom were no longer visible, having disappeared behind the side of the jury box, after clutching themselves and doubling over.

Me: Thank you, Mr. Harris. I have no further questions. Your witness, Ms. McAfee.

Although I knew it would be an exercise in futility, I expected her to attempt to cross-examine Mr. Harris. I was far from certain she would be able to control her laughter enough to pose any questions, but McAfee proved to be made of sterner stuff than I had thought. She set her face in an exaggerated expression of seriousness, and asked her first question.

ADA: Mr. Harris, isn't it a fact that when you went into the living room, you said, "What do I have to do, kill you?" to your wife?

Witness: No ma'am, I never did. Mrs. Lincoln lied to the police when she testified that I didn't live there, it was my house and Lauren didn't have no right to my Social Security, and she locked me out for no reason, because Mrs. Lincoln was telling her how to get my money.

ADA (looks away and snorts): Mr. Harris, please answer the question. On the day you were arrested, did you threaten your wife?

Witness: No, I did not, because we were married for two years and this Mrs. Lincoln is in the house when I never seen her before in my life, so how did I know she didn't have a knife when she sneaked up behind me and it's none of her business anyway?

This answer pushed poor Ms. McAfee over the edge. She laughed so hard that she was quite unable to form a single coherent word for a full minute.

I leaned over to compliment her cross-examination. "Great work, Jan," I whispered. "You have him on the run now."

She looked at me, then at the witness, then realizing that cross examining Harris was like trying to empty the sea with a fork; it was a complete waste of time. She sat down and said, "No more questions."

Then it was time to sum up. Since the prosecution has the burden of proving the defendant guilty, they get to go last, which meant that I went first, and had to anticipate the prosecution's arguments.

"Members of the jury, on behalf of my client, Ms. McAfee and Judge Mueller, I want to thank each and every one of you for taking time from your busy lives to perform what I consider to be the most important duty of citizenship, by sitting in judgement of a fellow citizen accused of a crime...

"Ms. McAfee will doubtless tell you that, if you believe Mrs. Lincoln's testimony, you will have no choice but to find George Harris guilty, and that you could only reach a different verdict if you decide that Mrs. Lincoln was lying. But that isn't exactly true, is it? You might have a reasonable doubt, even if, like me, you believed the witness was absolutely sincere, if you thought she was mistaken, honestly mistaken, about what happened...

"Ms. McAfee will urge you to look closely at Mrs. Lincoln's testimony, and I will ask you to do the same thing. But I want you to look at *all* of it, not just her testimony on direct examination. You will remember that when Ms. McAfee was questioning her, Mrs. Lincoln forgot to tell you that she had come up behind George Harris while he was arguing with his wife, and surprised him at what must have been a very difficult moment. She didn't remember until I reminded her of it on cross. So, Mrs. Lincoln confirmed George Harris' testimony that she had startled him, and this might have caused him to turn suddenly and make accidental contact with her, cause her to lose her balance, and fall. If you believe that she *might* have sustained her injuries that way, that would be enough for a reasonable doubt, and you could find Mr. Harris not guilty based solely on that testimony.

"But there's something else, something so simple and obvious that it creates an overwhelming doubt about the defendant's guilt, all by itself. During cross examination, I asked Mrs. Lincoln how much she weighed. She answered that she weighed around 360 pounds, about the same as she did back at the time of the incident...

"Mr. Harris, please stand up and let the jury take a look at you...Thank you, you can sit down...You can see that George Harris is not a very big man. I would say that he is about my height, 5 foot 7, and weighs a little more, maybe 170. You will also observe that he looks pretty strong, definitely stronger than me, anyway.

"Now keep the relative sizes of Edna Lincoln and George Harris in mind, while I read back a few questions and answers from Mrs. Lincoln's testimony on cross-examination.

Question (by me): So, you were just outside the dining room when you came up behind Mr. Harris, correct?

Witness: Yes.

Question: Then, you say, he turned around, grabbed you and walked you back to the dining room, then picked you up and threw you across the room to land on the table. Is that right?

Witness: Yes, sir, that's what he did.

Me: You said he threw you. Do you mean that your feet left the ground, and you flew through the air to the table?

Witness: Yes. He picked me up and threw me like a bag of laundry, and I landed on my back right on the table.

"Members of the jury, I think you will agree with me that Edna Lincoln's description of George Harris' actions is not believable. Your common sense will tell you that a 170-pound man, even an unusually strong one, is incapable of picking up a 360 woman and throwing her across a room. I think we can all agree that would be physically impossible.

"I suggest that, if you fit the believable pieces of Mrs. Lincoln's testimony together with what you heard from George Harris, you will find the most likely explanation: George Harris *did* cause her fall, but he did it *accidently*, and not intentionally. Remember that George Harris was in a state of extreme emotional stress after he came home to find himself locked out of his own house. Then, without any warning, his wife told him that he would have to find someplace else to live, which probably didn't help matters any. So, he entered through the cellar, went up the stairs and managed to force his way inside, despite Mrs. Lincoln's attempt to keep him out. As soon as he got into the dining room, he went over to his wife, not stopping to speak to Mrs. Lincoln, or even ask who she was. Both witnesses say that he didn't even seem to notice her at that time.

"Then he goes to confront his wife in the next room, and it isn't hard to imagine how confused and upset he must have been at that moment, when it seemed that his entire world was crashing down around his head. And just at the moment of maximum stress, Mrs. Lincoln, whose presence, whose very existence, he had probably forgotten, comes up behind him unnoticed, and shrieks "Jesus, Jesus, Jesus!" in his ear, from inches away. How did George Harris react? The same way you, or I, or almost anyone else would have. He was surprised, startled, shocked. He spun suddenly around to see who was behind him. We know from her own testimony that Edna Lincoln was very close to George Harris when this happened. She had to be close to shout in his ear the way she did. So, George's sudden movement would almost certainly have resulted in contact between him and Mrs. Lincoln. And it would not have taken a very hard bump to make elderly, 360-pound woman lose her balance and stagger backwards until she ran into something, in this case, the dining room table.

"And that, I submit, is how Mrs. Lincoln was injured by George Harris: accidentally. There was no intent to injure her, there was no assault, there was no crime. It was just a very unfortunate accident that ultimately was as much due to Mrs. Lincoln's actions as to George Harris'. Members of the jury, I will not ask you to do anything but your duty. If you find that the Commonwealth has proved George Harris' guilt beyond a reasonable doubt, your verdict should be guilty. But, if you find decide that they failed to meet this burden, and that you have a reasonable doubt about his guilt, I ask you to find Mr. Harris not guilty. After you have discussed the case and considered the evidence, I suggest that you will only be able to reach one conclusion, that the defendant, George Harris, is *not* guilty. Thank you."

McAfee did her usual professional job in her summation, reading from the medical records to remind the jury about the terrible injuries that had left Edna Lincoln bound to a wheelchair for the rest of her life. She urged the jurors to remember how the witness had given them such a detailed description of the assault by the defendant, and argued that the witness had either told them the exact truth or was an incredibly talented liar. She also pointed out that Mrs. Lincoln had no reason to accuse George Harris of attacking her if he had not done it, and concluded by asking the jury to find the defendant guilty.

I watched the faces of the jurors during the prosecutor's summation. They were definitely paying attention to her words, but I did not see any indication that they had been persuaded by them. Of course, that also didn't mean that they *hadn't* been persuaded either. I had guessed wrong about juries before.

Fifteen minutes later the jury was back, and we were listening to the foreman announce the verdict, "Not guilty."

It was a nice win, and the right outcome. I believed then (and still do,) that George Harris was innocent and had been wrongly convicted at his first trial. So, if justice was done, and in such an entertaining manner, why do I call it a Pyrrhic victory? Here's why: the sentence Judge Mueller had imposed on Harris after the first trial was 10 to 20 years. And how long did he have to wait in prison before the Supreme Court granted his appeal? *Eight years*, that's how long. Since he would have been paroled after he completed the 10-year minimum, the verdict at the second trial got him something less than two years off his time in prison, which doesn't come anywhere near righting the wrong that was done to an innocent man. Justice delayed is justice denied. Not an original thought, certainly, but still true.

*I wasn't too worried about an objection anyway, as the witness's words "Jesus, Jesus, Jesus," weren't actually hearsay. In the Pennsylvania Rules of Evidence (by Professors Leonard Packel and Anne Poulin, from whom I learned the law of evidence at Villanova Law School, by the way,) hearsay is defined in Rule 801 as, "An out-of-court statement offered to prove the truth of the matter asserted." In other words, in order for the statement to be hearsay, it must be offered for its *content,* and not for some other purpose. In this case, we were not offering Mrs. Lincoln's exclamations as evidence that the Savior was a witness or was otherwise personally involved in Commonwealth v. Harris. Instead, I was trying to show the effect her words had on my client, namely that they had startled him. Therefore, "Jesus, Jesus, Jesus!" was not hearsay, because it was offered for a permissible, non-hearsay purpose under Rule

801.2. I probably also could have gotten it admitted as an excited utterance under Rule 803.2. Remember, I *did* warn you there was some educational material in here.

Snapshot: The Monkey Trap

It is said that in South Asia, they trap monkeys by putting a banana at the bottom of a container with a neck that is wide enough to admit a monkey's empty hand, but too narrow for it to be taken out while holding the banana. The monkeys can free themselves at any time by just letting go of the banana, but apparently they hold on until they are captured. The expression "monkey trap" has come to mean any trap that depends on the victim's greed to work. Here is the story of a self-created monkey trap from early in my career.

One of the less pleasant jobs in the Brooklyn DA's office was a 24-hour shift in what was called the Investigations Unit, or sometimes, Special Investigations. Our most important duty in Investigations was called "riding." There were two riding assistants on duty at any time, and they had two jobs. First, whenever an arrest was made for one of the crimes on the list of designated felonies (murder, rape, kidnapping, the shooting of a policeman [not a shooting *by* one], and a few others), a riding assistant and camera operator would take a ride out to the precinct where the crime had occurred, to ensure there was probable cause to charge the suspect, interview witnesses and where appropriate, record their statements on video, prepare a complaint, and make sure evidence was properly preserved. I don't know why, but we were usually called on these cases between midnight and 2 AM, when the graveyard shift came on duty at the precinct. You can imagine how happy we were to be shaken awake (there was an old, ratty sofa we were allowed to sleep on while we were waiting,) to drag our weary carcasses out somewhere in the wilds of Brooklyn to ride a murder case.

We also went out on felony arrests for crimes not on the riding list. If a suspect was willing to talk, a riding assistant would be sent out with the camera man to record his statement. It was this latter duty that brought me out to the Coney Island headquarters of the 60th police district at 3 o'clock in the morning, to take a video statement from a suspect accused of burglary, for breaking into a cigar shop and removing property from the store without permission of the owner. (The police hadn't got in touch with the owner by the time I got there, but I judged that there was sufficient circumstantial evidence that the suspect lacked permission to meet the probable cause requirements.)

Once the suspect's Miranda rights were recorded for posterity, I started the interview. The suspect, a young, athletic-looking fellow, answered my questions with apparent candor, admitting that he had broken into the cigar shop by smashing the display window with a brick, then going inside and trying to force open the cash register with a crowbar. However, this was not one of your modern, flimsy, lightweight, electronic cash registers. This was a real, old-time model, built to survive being thrown from a fifth-floor window, or an atomic bomb, probably, and was equipped with an equally tough lock.

After trying and failing to pry open the massive cash register with his crowbar for what must have felt like a long time, the perp began to worry that he would be apprehended if he stayed at the scene for much longer. But having gone to the trouble of getting inside the store, he was unwilling to walk away empty-handed. He felt certain that given a little intimate time alone with the cash register, he would find a way to overcome its shyness and persuade it to open for him. So he decided to transfer the entire operation to a safe location, by picking up the cash register and carrying it out of the store.

The cash register had been recovered by the arresting officers, who brought it to the precinct, giving me a chance to see it for myself. I had no doubt that it weighed well in excess of 100 pounds, and I was impressed that this slight-looking fellow could even lift it, let alone carry it anywhere. But his surprising strength only made matters worse for him. He would have been better off if he had been a 90-pound weakling, who wasn't strong enough to carry such a heavy object.

Two police officers saw the perp exiting the cigar shop with the cash register in his arms and gave chase. The suspect had a half-block lead on his pursuers, and probably could have outrun them, if he had simply abandoned his prize. But, like a monkey who is captured because he will not let go of the banana, the burglar was brought low by his own greed. Rather than abandoning his prize, he tried to escape while burdened with the loot, and was easily overtaken and apprehended by the police, an object lesson in the danger of unbridled materialism.

As the interview progressed, my gaze became more and more drawn to a lump developing over the suspect's right eye. It started out perhaps half the diameter of a golf ball, and grew steadily during the interview, until it was nearly the size of a tangerine. After he finished answering my last question (or what should have been the last one, anyway,) I was so transfixed by the sight that I asked *another* question.

"So, how did you get that lump?" I asked, quite unnecessarily, as with a little thought, I could have easily deduced the answer myself.

He scowled, and pointed his finger at the proximate cause, the older of the two arresting officers. "The sergeant over there did it," he said, glaring. "After...

The sergeant jumped up from his chair like a jack-in-the-box, shaking his head and loudly protesting his innocence.

I waved him back down. "Let him finish his answer, please. If you still want to respond for the record, you can do it after I'm finished taking this statement, Sergeant." The younger cop put a restraining hand on his colleague's forearm, and whispered something I couldn't make out. The sergeant sat down again, muttering under his breath.

"Go on," I said, returning to the suspect. Having opened this can of worms, I didn't think I could just drop it as if it had never happened. "You were saying that it happened after something, correct?"

He nodded. "It was after they put on the cuffs. They had me up against a wall. I was just standing there, doing nothing...when the sergeant puts his hand on the back of my head and slams me into the wall!" As he spoke these last few words, his voice rose and he scowled at object of his accusation.

"How do you know it was the sergeant, if he was behind you?" I asked.

"Cause I could see the young guy," he answered. "He was squatting on the ground next to me, looking at the cash register."

At this, the junior officer started to say something, but I waved him to silence. "Is there anything else you would like to tell me about what happened tonight?" I asked in the hope of wrapping up the statement without any further surprises.

"Nah," he said, shaking his head, "that's all I got to say."

The younger cop told the sergeant to take the prisoner back to his cell while he told me what "really" happened, which I thought was a little strange. I would have expected the more experienced one to come up with an explanation, especially since he was the one accused of roughing up the prisoner.

"Listen, Mr. Heller," the young cop said ,after his partner left the interview room with the suspect, "that mutt [cop slang for a criminal suspect or any lowlife in general] is lying. He was giving us all kinds of lip, calling us pigs, motherf--ers, every name you can think of, and he wouldn't stop until I pushed his face into that wall."

I thought about that for a few seconds. It *might* have happened that way, I supposed, but I couldn't think of any motive for the "mutt" to blame the sergeant, if the other cop had done it. On the other hand, it occurred to me that there might be a very good reason for the young cop to lie to protect his partner, and I had an educated guess about that reason might be.

"Do you know if the sergeant has ever been written up for, oh, I don't know, abusing prisoners?" I asked. When he looked down at the floor and didn't answer right away, I added, "Off the record, of course."

He hesitated at first, then bobbed his head once. "Yeah. Something like that."

"Maybe he was even suspended for it?" I guessed, now pretty sure I was on the right track.

"Mr. Heller," he said urgently, "the Sarge is eligible for retirement with a full pension in a couple months. But if he gets in trouble again, it might ..." He trailed off.

I shrugged. "If you want me to write it up the way you told me, I will," I said. "It's no skin off my ass. Chances are there won't be an investigation." He was obviously relieved when he heard that I wasn't going to be a problem. "But if there is," I added, "you understand that *you'll* be the one facing a disciplinary action?"

He nodded again. "Yeah, I understand," he said. "I guess I'll take my chances."

I regret that I have to leave this story unfinished, because I never heard anything more about it, so I can't tell you if either cop was punished for bouncing the monkey trap burglar's coconut off a brick wall.

Snapshot: Tuna Fish Is *Not* Spaghetti

When we weren't "riding" in the Investigations unit, we were assigned to ECAB, to be available if any of the perps, skells, or mutts wanted to make a statement. ECAB was filthy and crowded, but you got used to that part soon enough. What wasn't so easy to accept was the boredom. We were stuck in the place for eight hours, and the only break from the monotony was when someone unwisely agreed to make a statement.

[Well, there was an hour dinner break, which we could use to stroll over to the only business open after midnight in that urban jungle, a restaurant called Senior's. Since the only people around at that time were either law enforcement professionals or their quarry, Senior's was by necessity the eatery of choice for both groups. I invented a motto for the restaurant, which I thought they should have put up on the big neon sign in front: "Senior's: Where Cops and Perps Meet."]

One night, when I was working the midnight-to-eight shift, I decided to become proactive (or maybe just "active," I'm not sure what the difference is,) and instead of waiting around for some poor slob to answer questions for the camera, I would poke around until I found a volunteer.

I soon found myself in a part of the building I had never seen before. Down at the far end of a hallway was an open door, with light streaming from the other side. Also coming from the doorway was the sound of multiple voices.

I came cautiously up to the doorway, and stepped into a room. The room contained a cage made of steel bars, 18 or 20 feet on a side. Inside this cage were, oh, I don't know, maybe 100 prisoners. No, I know it couldn't have been that many, but it sure seemed like it. Because, when the prisoners saw me, they immediately began screaming at the top of their lungs. It wasn't easy to make out individual words in the uproar, but I gathered that they wanted to be released.

There was a cop in the room, sitting behind a desk. When the screaming began, he got up and sauntered towards me. "Can I help you, counselor?" he asked.

I declined the offer, and hastily backed away, and that was the last time I went looking for statements at ECAB.

From time to time, one of us would get a memorable statement. One of my colleagues recorded this interview with a murder suspect.

Suspect: We was playing cards up in his apartment, and he said, "I'm hungry. You got anything to eat?" I said "Yeah, I got a can of spaghetti. You can have that." So we went down to my apartment, and I showed him where the spaghetti was in the cabinet. So, instead of taking the spaghetti, he takes a can of tuna fish, then goes over and starts opening it. I said, "Take the spaghetti. You can't have my tuna fish." He don't pay no attention to me." [The suspect is grows increasingly excited.] He just smiles and keeps right on opening my tuna fish. So, I get a knife out of the drawer, and I stab him. [Suspect suddenly stops and looks at his feet. When he faces the camera again, he looks and sounds genuinely contrite.] "I killed him. I shouldn't have done that.: [Looks down again. Then he looks up and shouts] "But I *told* him not to take my tuna fish!"

Eight: Driving Around in a Car That Nobody Owns, Part One

The professor I had for Property Law, Wills, Trusts and Estates, and related subjects at Villanova Law School was the late Leonard Levin [real name]. Like most law professors, he was a very intelligent man. But that does not mean that he was particularly adept at expressing himself. On the contrary, he was notable for the way he tortured the language. This many years later, I can recall only two of his numerous offenses against English, one of which is relevant here.

To describe a bad situation where there was no good solution, he would say "You'd be up a tree without a paddle." When he gave an example of something that was impossible, he would say it was, "like driving around in a car that nobody owns." I only wish Professor Levin had still been alive when I tried Commonwealth v. Jenkins, a case that revolved around a car that nobody owned.

Jamaal Jenkins was charged with Aggravated Assault, (Attempted) Robbery, Theft of a Motor Vehicle, Receiving Stolen Property and Criminal Conspiracy to commit all of the above. The facts as alleged by the prosecution witnesses were unusual enough to make most ADAs take a closer look at the evidence, and at least consider offering a misdemeanor plea rather than going to trial.

But Tom Eckert was not "most ADAs," as I discovered when I approached him to point out some of the strange allegations made by his witnesses.

"Are you really *sure* about this case?" I asked. "Doesn't it bother you that the kid…" [by whom I meant the teenager Bruce Harrold] "…told the cops that my client made him go home to fetch the *title* of the car he had stolen? I mean, have you ever heard of a car thief demanding the title, or for that matter, the victim getting it for him? Doesn't that strike you as a *little* funny?"

Apparently not. Eckert gave me an irritated look, and said, "Your client, Mr. Heller, was arrested while he was removing the steering wheel of the car at *midnight*." He emphasized the final word, as if that evidence of a guilty conscience clinched the case right then and there.

I was tempted to say nothing and let him argue that to the jury, but I decided that would be too cruel, even for me. I leaned over to point at the time of arrest on the 75-49. "Actually, he was arrested at 12*PM*, otherwise known as 'noon' or 'midday,'" I said. "And was doing it at the same place where he got the car, which was two blocks away from the Harrold house. Doesn't that sound like he believed he owned the car?"

Although the props had been knocked out from under the theory that Mr. Jenkins' guilt was proved by his surreptitious behavior (since there was nothing especially suspicious about working on a car parked on the street in broad daylight,) Eckert's belief in the righteousness of his cause was not affected.

"The offer hasn't changed," he snapped. "Does he want it or not? Because when he's convicted, Judge Steele will give him a lot more than that."

Since the offer was 2 ½ to 5 years imprisonment, Jenkins had no record, and the case, in my estimation, consisted mostly of holes, I thought Eckert's evaluation was far more optimistic than was warranted by the facts. "No, he's not interested," I said, which I knew, because Jenkins had already rejected the offer. "I guess he'll have to take his chances."

Nonetheless, crappy as the case was, there was some small sense in what the ADA had said. Judge Marjorie Steele was as well known for her draconian sentences as she was for her Commonwealth bias. She had been a prosecutor before taking the bench, and had never gotten over it. She still believed that the only good verdict was a guilty verdict, and she was not about let a guilty defendant (which is to say, *any* defendant) get away with his crime, if she could do anything about it. If you have read this far, it probably goes without saying, but just in case anyone is wondering, I will tell you that Judge Steele and I got along like a cobra and a mongoose.

Anyway, we got through the jury selection process with no more than a few minor skirmishes, and started the trial. The first witness for the Commonwealth was Bruce Harrold. Mr. Eckert elicited the date, time and place and had the witness identify the defendant. Then we were off.

Eckert: On the day of this incident, did you have any occasion to see the defendant?

Witness: Yeah. We was both down at the playground.

Eckert: And what were you doing down at the playground?

Witness: Me and him was…

Eckert: By "him," do you mean the defendant, Jamaal Jenkins?

Witness: Yeah.

Eckert: Please refer to the defendant by name from now on, for the court reporter. Okay?

Witness: Yeah, okay. Anyways, we was shooting hoops for a while, then he…I mean the defendant…asked me if I wanted to sell my car to him.

Eckert: Where was the car?

Witness: My father had just gave me the car, and I drove it over to the playground. It was parked at the curb right there.

Eckert: And when he asked you if you would sell him the car, what did you say?

Witness: I said, no, I don't want to.

Eckert: And then what happened?

Witness: He got …*Jamaal* got real mad, and he pulled out a gun, and said, "Gimme the keys, I'm taking the car."

Eckert: Were those his exact words: "Gimme the keys, I'm taking the car?"

Witness: Well, I'm not sure. It was *something* like that.

Eckert: And what happened after he took the keys from you at gunpoint?

Witness: He asked me where was the title to the car, 'cause he wanted it.

Eckert: And what did you say?

Witness: I told him it was back at my house, so he said to go get it.

Eckert: And did you?

Witness: Yeah. I went home and got the title, and brought it back to the playground.

Eckert: And what did you do with the title?

Witness: I gave it to Jamaal.

Seemingly well satisfied with this bizarre story, Mr. Eckert smirked at me and told the judge, "I have no more questions, Your Honor."

The latter glowered down at me. "Do you have any questions for this witness, Mr. Heller," she asked.

"Yes, Your Honor, I do," said, doing my best to ignore the judicial scowl that met this reply.

Bruce Harrold's testimony here was even less plausible than his earlier testimony at the preliminary hearing. I did not expect it to hold up very well under cross examination.

Me: You knew Jamaal Jenkins from around the neighborhood, before this incident, didn't you?

Witness: Yeah, I seen him around.

Me: In fact, you were friendly with each other before this incident, weren't you?

Witness: I knew him, yeah.

Me: And he had never pulled a gun on you, or threatened you in any way before this, did he?

Witness: No.

Me: In fact, this was the first time you ever saw him with a gun, isn't that right?

Witness: Yeah, I guess so.

Me: So, when you saw him at the playground, you challenged him to a game of basketball, didn't you?

Witness: No. He asked me.

Me: And you agreed to play one-on-one with him, didn't you?

Witness: Yeah.

Me: And either Jamaal or you suggested you play for money, correct?

[My client had told me about this bet, which explained a lot about Bruce Harrold's testimony.]

Witness: Jamaal wanted to bet.

Me: And how much did Jamaal offer to bet?

Witness: $500

Me: Did he actually have $500 on him?

Witness: Yeah. He pulled this wad out of his pocket and showed me.

Me: And you wanted to win that $500, didn't you?

Witness: Yeah, I guess so.

Me: But you didn't have any money to put up, did you?

Witness: No.

Me: So, you put up the car as your stake against Jamaal's $500, didn't you?

[Witness does not answer.]

Me: Please answer my question, Mr. Harrold. You bet the car, and when you lost the game to Jamaal, you had to give him the keys? Isn't that what happened?

Witness: (mumbles something inaudible.)

Me: Speak up, Mr. Harrold. We can't hear you.

Witness: Yeah.

Me: Yeah, you lost the car gambling with Jamaal?

Witness: Yeah.

Me: And when you told Mr. Eckert that you gave the car keys to Jamaal because he pulled a gun on you, that wasn't true, was it?

Witness: No.

Me: And that bet was also the reason you went home and got the title for Jamaal, wasn't it?

Witness: Yeah.

Me: And the truth is that you never saw Jamaal with a gun that day, that he never threatened you, and that he didn't steal the car, the keys or the title, isn't it?

Witness: Yeah.

Court: Are you about finished with this witness, Mr. Heller?

Me: Almost, Your Honor. I just have a few more questions.

Me: You made up the story about Jamaal having a gun when your father asked you what happened to the car, isn't that right?

Eckert: Objection.

Court: Sustained.

Me: Well, you didn't call the police when you got home, did you?

Eckert: Objection.

Court: Sustained. [ominously] Move on, Mr. Heller.

Me: Your father was the one who called the police, because you told him you had been robbed, isn't that what happened?

Court: Objection sustained. Counsel will approach.

[At sidebar] Court: Mr. Heller, if you want to be held in contempt, I'll be glad to oblige you. This cross-examination is over. Return to your places.

She's no fun at all, I thought, as we returned to our respective counsel tables. As it happened, I did not particularly want to be held in contempt. For one thing, there was a substantial fine involved ($1500,) and considering that I only expected to make $1500 on this case, I really couldn't afford it. Besides, I would be able to make the same points when I cross-examined the other complaining witness, Bruce's father, Calvin Harrold.

158

Snapshot: Own Goal

When a cop testifies to something that he really doesn't remember (which many of them do as a matter of course,) he can find himself in an embarrassing position. Sometimes, a cop's lies can result in the soccer equivalent of kicking the ball into your own net, an "own goal." My client was the beneficiary of a wrong-way cop on an otherwise routine narcotics case.

I was representing one of two co-defendants on charges of Possession with Intent to Deliver and Criminal Conspiracy at a preliminary hearing at the 35th Police District at Broad and Champlost Streets. (Most preliminary hearings take place in either the police precinct where the crime occurred, or a nearby precinct.) The co-defendant and co-counsel were not present on this occasion.

There was nothing unusual about the factual allegations. According to the complaint, the two defendants had been selling drugs on a street corner near the Fern Rock subway station. My client was approached by various persons who engaged in brief conversations with him, then handed him U.S. currency. Whereupon, my client would signal to his colleague, who would remove one or more small objects from the bumper of a parked car, and hand the objects to the individual who had given money to my client. Two of the buyers were arrested and found to be in possession of green-topped glass vials containing alleged cocaine-base. Recovered from the bumper of the car was a sandwich bag containing 26 green-topped glass vials, which were found to contain alleged cocaine-base (this allegation was based on field testing of the substance in question. There had not been time to perform the official lab test, but the field test was enough to make out probable cause.)

So far, so good. The Commonwealth now called the arresting officer, who testified in the usual bored manner about his observations. To my considerable surprise, however, he stated that the other, absent defendant had collected the money, and my client doled out the narcotics to the customers. I fully expected the ADA to steer his cop back in the right direction, but he didn't seem to notice that his witness had the ball tucked under his arm and sprinting to the wrong end-zone.

On cross-examination, I pretended to be skeptical of the cop's ability to observe the sales: "How far away were you from the defendant?" "Were there any obstructions to your view?" "Isn't it true that the lighting was too poor for you to see anything?" (The answer to the last was that the entire operation took place directly below a streetlamp which illuminated everything and everyone perfectly.) The more I tried to cast doubt on cop's story, the more he insisted that he had told nothing but the exact truth.

I rested, then moved to discharge the case, pointing out that the officer had gotten the identification of the two suspects backwards, swearing that my client had been giving out the drugs, while in the complaint, he said it was the other defendant.

When the judge asked the ADA if he had any argument, the poor fellow just shook his head. The judge dismissed the charges for lack of evidence, then told the young prosecutor, "You do realize your office will not be able to recharge either defendant after this?"

[Normally, if a case is dismissed at a preliminary hearing, the prosecutor can pull up its socks and try again. But in this case, they were stuck with the sworn testimony of the arresting officer, and there was no way to fix the damage.]

GOOOOOOOOOOAL! Defense wins, one-nil!

Snapshot: Judge for a Day

I was always looking for ways to get a few more crumbs. One source of income was to sit on a panel at the Arbitration Center, and hear civil cases. Philadelphia's arbitration system was one of the first in the country, and is a model for other jurisdictions with impossibly long lists in the civil courts, or so I am told. In Philadelphia, if the claim is less than $50,000, the case is sent to the Arb Center, where it will be heard by a panel of three lawyers, instead of a judge and/or jury in a Common Pleas courtroom. If either litigant is dissatisfied with the result, he or she may appeal the panel's decision to be heard by a real judge.

However, since there is almost certain to be a lengthy delay before an appeal can get a trial date in Common Pleas (two to three years, and even longer during the Covid siege), the parties normally accept the decision of the arbitrators, even if they're not happy with it. (As might be expected, at least one side is almost always dissatisfied with the verdict, the only exception being when both are.)

The arbitration system handles roughly 90 percent of the civil lawsuits filed in Philadelphia, and relieves the overburdened courts of this huge volume of cases. Even with this help, the waiting time for major cases (that is, for claims over $50,000) is still three to five years. One can only imagine what it would be without compulsory arbitration.

Most of the lawyers who sit on the panels consider it public service, as it only pays $200 a day. To me, $200 for a few hours work was nothing to be sneezed at, so I signed up for the Arb Center as often as possible, and put my name on the emergency counsel list, as being available to fill in if one of the scheduled panelists didn't show. When other work was particularly slow, I would even call the Arb Center to ask if they needed anybody that day, instead of waiting for them to call me.

Usually, neither of my fellow arbitrators wanted the responsibility of being head of the panel, which entailed ruling on objections and making sure the trial followed the same rules as in court. A lot of them were not trial attorneys, and so were unfamiliar with courtroom procedure and the rules of evidence, and they were happy to avoid the additional responsibility.

I, on the other hand, would have been in danger of falling asleep during some of the cases, if I didn't have something to think about other than the tedious presentations that were standard fare in arbitration. You see, the big firms give their arbitration cases to their newest, least experienced litigation associates, because if they screwed up, it wouldn't hurt the firm financially. As might be expected, these greenhorns would often make a pig's breakfast out of their cases, simply through lack of experience. Likewise, a surprising number of veteran lawyers for whom car accidents, slip-and-fall suits and the like were their bread and butter, were remarkably ineffectual as well. I can't say for sure why, but I suspect this was because, in spite of their long years of experience, many of them had hardly tried any cases, as they were used to settling instead of going to trial.

Until approximately 2000 or 2001, insurance carriers would routinely settle small personal injury claims---even cases that were dubious or downright suspicious---just to get rid of them. It was thought that it was cheaper to pay bogus injury claims (as long as they weren't too big,) than to pay attorneys to fight them in court. This practice combined with the contingent fee system to create a veritable Disneyland for dishonest lawyers and doctors.

For those of you who are not familiar with the unique American contingent fee system, a brief explanation is in order. While most lawyers charge a fixed hourly rate or a flat fee for each case, lawyers for plaintiffs in personal injury, medical malpractice, and other private lawsuits are compensated with a percentage of the recovery, if any. The client doesn't have any up-front expenses. This is justified as a way of providing legal services to people injured in accidents who, like many criminal defendants, can't afford to hire a lawyer. (As it happens, there is a substantial overlap between the two groups.)

The assumed benefit to society, however, is outweighed by the rampant corruption created by the contingent fee system. It has generated networks of lawyers, doctors, chiropractors, physical therapists, and other allied medical professionals dependent on income from negligence cases, while the medical professionals, all too often, base their diagnoses and treatment what plaintiff counsel needs than what the actual injuries are. The lawyers, naturally, do all they can to encourage personal injury claims, advertising how much money they have made for their clients on billboards, television, and radio.

With such encouragement, it is not surprising that there are so many lawsuits based on exaggerated or completely false injuries. There are, after all, a *lot* of personal injury attorneys, and they can't afford to turn down cases merely because the potential client wasn't actually injured. There's always somebody willing to take on even the most implausible claims. And, by the same token, there are always physicians who can find cervical sprain and strain, and other hard-to-diagnose soft tissue injuries in patients sent to them by the PI lawyers, doctors who, like the attorneys, are paid out the plaintiff's award. Since damages in garden variety personal injury cases are usually based on the number of weeks the plaintiff was treated for his injuries, certain PI doctors are willing to continue treatment long after any need for them has passed, or produce detailed records of treatments that never took place. The latter practices are insurance fraud, a felony, but that has not prevented them from being endemic to personal injury law. I far preferred to work with good, honest criminals.

As I said, until around 2000, insurance companies were unwilling participants in this dirty game. However, near the turn of the millennium, a consortium of insurance companies commissioned a study to see whether settling these nuisance cases really was the most economical way to handle them. To the surprise of the insurers and the dismay of the personal injury bar, the study concluded that the insurance companies had been doing exactly the opposite of what they should have. The most cost-effective way, according to this study, was to settle nothing and fight everything. So, around 2001 or so, the insurance companies stopped disposing of nuisance suits with small cash settlements, and started forcing the plaintiffs to put up a case in court or withdraw their claim. This new policy also had the virtue of discouraging the better personal injury lawyers from taking some of the really bad cases in the first place. I suspect this was the main reason we started to see so many unprepared, bumbleheaded attorneys in the Arb Center at this time.

I remember in particular hearing an accident case in which the defendant was a member of an outlaw motorcycle club. The plaintiff's attorney spoke and acted as if he was the second coming of Louis Nizer. In fact, the poor fellow was a victim of the Dunning-Kruger effect, which describes people so incompetent that they are incapable of understanding how incompetent they really are.

Just before this lawyer began his cross of the defendant, he said, "I have a motion for the admission of a *crimens falsi* conviction." This refers to crimes involving dishonesty or falsehood, and is an exception to the usual rule that a witness may not be impeached by prior bad acts, such as criminal convictions, adultery, drug abuse, and so forth (608.2 PA Rules of Evidence.) However, if the defendant in a criminal case chooses to testify, his credibility can be attacked with evidence of a prior conviction for a crime involving falsehood or dishonesty, and this applies to *any* witness in a civil case (609 PA Rules of Evidence.) Examples of *crimens falsi* offenses are forgery, embezzlement, theft, burglary, and receiving stolen property. Crimes of violence, such as murder, assault, or rape, are not admissible under this exception. I had just finished writing a short brief on this subject for one of my cases, so I was very familiar with the law in this area.

"Okay," I said. "What is your proffer?"

The plaintiff's attorney moved up to the table in the front of the room where we arbitrators were sitting, and handed each of us a piece of paper. "This defendant was convicted in 1994 of a violation of the Uniform Firearms Act, Title 18 Section 6106, possession of an unlicensed handgun," he announced triumphantly.

"Sorry, counselor," I said, "motion denied. That's not *crimens falsi*."

I was able to be categorical about this, because in the above-mentioned brief, I had used a Supreme Court case that *specifically cited* possession of a firearm without a license as an example of a crime that was *not* admissible under Rule 609.

The attorney bristled. "Yes, it is," he insisted.

"All right," I said, "then show me the case you are relying on." Naturally, he didn't, in fact, couldn't, because no such case existed.

"I didn't bring any cases," he ground out through clenched jaws.

"No?" I asked. "Why not?"

"Because," he answered, only just keeping at bay his anger at my hopeless ignorance of the law,

"I didn't think I'd need a case for something so *obvious*."

"Well, I don't want to be unreasonable," I told him. I looked at my watch. "It's almost 12, so if my fellow panelists have no objection, why don't we break for lunch right now...," I turned to address the attorney again, "and you'll have a chance to pop over to the law library and get a case to show me when we return at 1:30. How does that sound?"

After lunch, when all the necessary parties had returned to court, I asked the plaintiff's attorney if he could now provide the panel with a case on the issue we had been discussing before the break.

He made a sour face. "No," he said, a little brusquely, I thought.

I could have just let it drop right there, but I was enjoying myself too much to pass up an opportunity to turn the knife. I smiled sweetly and asked, "So, do you have any further argument, or will you be withdrawing the motion?"

He glared at me in undisguised loathing, which was hardly a good way to ingratiate himself with a judge who would be deciding his case. "The motion is withdrawn," he said, as sullen as a schoolboy being kept in after class.

"Very good," I said. "I believe you were about to cross-examine the defendant, so why don't we start there?"

*

The absolute worst decision to defend a civil case instead of settling that I ever heard as an arbitrator, was a Lemon Law suit brought by a young couple against General Motors. Ironically, the plaintiffs absolutely loved GM, believed, in the face of all evidence to contrary, that American-made vehicles were the best in the world, and that GM was the best of them all. They traded in their GMC truck and bought a new one every two years. In short, they were two of GM's biggest fans.

Until, that is, they bought a 2005 Sierra pick-up at a Philadelphia dealership. A few months after they purchased it, the truck started to have a serious mechanical problem: the engine would just shut down at unpredictable moments, for no reason the owners could see. This happened at least once while they were driving at high speed on the turnpike, creating a very dangerous situation.

The truck was under warranty, so they brought it back to the dealership where they had purchased it for repairs. The dealer's mechanics examined the truck, but couldn't find any cause for the problem. So, they made some minor adjustments, gave it back to the customers and told them the problem was fixed and it wouldn't happen again.

But it did happen again, of course, because it *hadn't* been fixed. The problem hadn't even been diagnosed. So, the young couple brought the Sierra back again…and again…and again. You might expect that, at some point, these customers would get sick and tired of taking their rolling junk pile back to the shop, but you would be wrong. Instead, GM told the young couple, those naïve, trusting customers, that since their mechanics couldn't find anything wrong with their truck, there *wasn't* anything wrong with it, and the dealer would not do any more work on it.

This left the plaintiffs with no choice. They found a lawyer, and brought a suit under the Pennsylvania Lemon Law. This law requires car dealers to return the purchase price of any new car that has serious mechanical problems within the first 12 months that cannot be fixed after three attempts.

As I listened to the plaintiffs testify, I grew steadily more amazed at the dealer and GM. Why, I wondered, did the company not simply give these people a new truck before they were sued? The public relations value of a gesture like that would certainly have more than made up for the immediate monetary loss, and I had the feeling that even after all they had been through, the plaintiffs still wanted to own a GM product.

Having let the matter go so far, GM still could have surrendered gracefully, settled the lawsuit, and given the couple their money back. While this wouldn't have done the brand much good, it probably wouldn't have hurt it too much, either.

But no. Rather than admitting that they had sold these customers a defective product, the dealership and GM threw down the gauntlet and dug in for a fight to the finish. They brought in the GM supervisor of mechanics for the entire northeast United States to examine the truck and write a report denying that there was anything wrong with their truck. Their lawyers prepared an elaborate 50-page brief that included detailed records of all the attempts to repair the truck by the dealership. They put the regional supervisor on the stand to insist that *the truck was all right*! I had to shake my head in disbelief.

When the defense finally rested, and before GM's attorney started her closing argument, I asked, "Counselor, what is your theory of this case? Are we supposed to believe that the plaintiffs maliciously made up this story about their truck shutting down to ruin your client? Or is it your position that they are delusional, and they imagined the whole thing?"

She didn't answer. (And really, what could she have said?) Instead, she gave me a dirty look, and launched into her argument. It took us about five minutes to find in favor of the plaintiffs.

Postscript: In 2022, GM settled a $121 million class action suit that accused the company of installing defective ignition switches in GMC trucks, including the Sierra. The defect would cause the engines of trucks equipped with the defective part to suddenly stop. In the course of the litigation, it was discovered that GM knew about the defective switches as early as 2003, but covered it up, so the company would not have to pay to recall the vehicles and replace the switches.

Nine: Driving Around in a Car Nobody Owns, Part Two

After the fiasco of Bruce Harrold's testimony, Mr. Eckart's remaining hopes rested on the shoulders of Bruce's father, Calvin Harrold. The witness stated that he was 61 years old, and had lived in the same North Philadelphia neighborhood for over 30 years.

Eckert: Mr. Harrold, on the morning of this incident, did anything unusual happen?

Witness: Yes. I come home from work, and I see that my son's car isn't parked in front of the house where it was supposed to be.

Eckert: When you say your son's car, do you mean Bruce's car?

Witness: Yeah. It's a '77 Buick his older brother gave me.

Eckert: When you saw that the car was missing, what did you do?

Witness: I asked him...Bruce...what did he do with it?

Eckert: And what did he say?

[I could have objected here, but I wanted the jury to hear the story Bruce made up to keep his father from finding out he had gambled the car away.]

Witness: He said some kid who lives around the corner held him up, and stole it. He said it was parked over by the playground.

Eckert: So, what did you do?

Witness: I said, your brother gave me that car, and I gave it to you, and no little punk is gonna steal it from us. Then I got a baseball bat and went around to the playground to talk to this kid who took our car.

Eckert: And when you got to the playground, what happened?

Witness: There was three of them around the car. That one… [points at defendant] was inside the car, doing something to the steering wheel.

Eckert: For the record, indicating the defendant, Jamaal Jenkins. Go on, Mr. Harrold. Please continue.

Witness: His two friends were sitting…

Me: Objection. There has been no evidence that these two men were friends of the defendant.

Court: Overruled. You may continue your answer.

Witness: They were sitting on the hood yakking with him…the defendant.

Eckert: What happened next?

Witness: I come over to the car and I said, "What are you doing with Bruce's car?"

Eckart: And what did the defendant, Jamaal Jenkins do?

Witness: He laughed and said, "It's mine now. I won it off him. I got the title and everything." Then he shakes the title at me.

Eckert: And then what happened?

Witness: I said, "Boy, you better get out that car right now, if you know what's good for you."

Eckert: And how did he respond?

Witness: He didn't. He just went back to doing whatever he was doing before I got there.

Eckert: Then what happened?

Witness: One of the other kids says, "You better run along back home, old head, or you might get hurt." Then he pulls a gun out from behind, from his pants, I guess, points it at me and fires.

Eckert: Were you struck by the bullet?

Witness: Nah. He wasn't just trying to hit me. He was pointing down at the ground, trying to scare me.

Eckert: And were you scared?

Witness: Yeah. I'd have to be pretty stupid not to be scared, when somebody's shooting off a gun like that.

Eckert: So, what did you do?

Witness: I went back to my house and called the cops.

Eckert: What did you tell them?

Witness: The same thing I told you just now.

[Eckert returns to his table and takes a pink sheet of paper from his file.]

Eckert: I ask this be marked Commonwealth Exhibit One for identification.

Me: May I see it?

Eckert: [coming over to show me the exhibit.] You already have this, Mr. Heller. It was supplied as part of discovery.

Me: Okay.

Eckert: [returning to the witness.] Mr. Harrold, I am showing you this document that has been marked C-1. Do you know what it is?

Witness: Yes. That's the title to my son's Buick.

Eckert: Is this what you saw the defendant Jamal Jenkins waving at you when you saw him in the car?

Witness: I think so. It's the same color, but I didn't get close enough to see if it was that exact paper.

Eckert: No further questions. Your witness.

I had prepared some questions for cross, naturally, but the witness's answers had inspired a few new ones.

Me: Mr. Harrold, you said that after you talked to your son, Bruce, you got a baseball bat, and went over to the playground looking for Jamaal Jenkins. Is that right?

Witness: Yes.

Me: Why did you bring a baseball bat? Were you planning to organize a pick-up baseball game?

Eckert: Objection.

Court: Sustained.

Me: Why did you take a bat along with you when you went to talk to my client?

Witness: I wanted him to know I was serious.

Me: You brought the bat to threaten Mr. Jenkins, if he didn't give you the car. Isn't that why you brought it?

Witness: Yes. I figured, if he don't want to listen, I should have something to get his attention.

Me: When he didn't get out of the car after you told him to, you went over to the car, and threatened him with the bat, didn't you?

Witness: I didn't *threaten* him, no.

Me: But you did raise the bat over your head when you approached the car, didn't you?

Witness: I didn't do it to threaten anybody. I just wanted to get his attention.

Me: But you did raise the bat up over your head as you approached the car, right?

Witness: Yes.

Me: Is it fair to say that Jamaal Jenkins was in the car when you arrived at the playground, and that he remained there until you left?

Witness: As far as I saw, yes. He didn't get out of the car.

Me: And you never saw him with a gun or any kind of weapon in his hand, did you?

Witness: No. I didn't see him with a gun.

Me: The only thing you saw him holding was that pink paper, right?

Witness: As far as I can remember, yes.

Me: My client never spoke to the two other men the entire time you were at the playground. True?

Witness: Well, I didn't hear him say anything to them.

Me: Mr. Jenkins did not give either of the others any orders, did he?

Witness: Not that I heard.

Me: He didn't give either of the two men on the hood of the car any directions, did he?

Witness: What do you mean, directions?

Me: He didn't tell them to do anything, did he?

Witness: No.

Me: Specifically, Mr. Jenkins did not say anything to the man who pulled out the gun, did he?

Witness: If he did, I didn't hear him.

Me: You told Mr. Eckert that you didn't think the man who fired the shot was trying to hit you, that he was just trying to scare you, right?

Witness: Yes.

Me: And is that because he was not aiming the gun at you, but was pointing it down at the street?

Witness: That's one reason.

Me: And is another reason because you were only a few feet away from him when he fired that shot, so it would have been almost impossible for him to miss, unless he wanted to.

Witness: Yes.

Me: But you told Mr. Eckert you were scared. If you didn't believe he was trying to shoot you, why were you scared?

Witness: 'Cause he might've hit me by accident, if a bullet bounced off the pavement the wrong way, maybe. Guns are dangerous.

Me: I agree. Now one final thing, Mr. Harrold.

[I turn around to take C-1 from the evidence table behind me.]

Me: I'm showing you what has already been marked as Commonwealth Exhibit 1.

[I hand C-1 to the witness.]

Me: You told Mr. Eckhart that this is the title to the car allegedly stolen by Mr. Jenkins. Will you please read what is printed at the very top of the paper.

[I lean over the witness box to point to the line I want him to read.]

Witness: It says "Application for Transfer of Ownership of Motor Vehicle."

Me: Right. It doesn't say it's the title to a 1977 Buick Regal, or the title to any car at all, does it?

Witness: I don't know.

Me: It is just an application to *transfer* a title, not an actual title, correct?

Witness: [Looking over the paper before answering.] I guess that's right.

Me: And when you look at that form, you can see that most of the spaces are blank. It was never completed, was it?

Witness: That's how it looks.

Me: Now I want you to look very carefully at that application to transfer a title, and see if your name, the name of your son Bruce, or your older son's name is anywhere on that form.

Witness: [Studies the exhibit.]

Me: Well, do you see the name of anyone in your family on that form?

Witness: No. The only name on here is Latisha Harris. She was my son Alan's girlfriend. He bought the car from her.

Me: Do you have any official document from the Commonwealth of Pennsylvania, such as a title or registration that proves that you, your sons, or anyone else in your family has legal ownership of the 1977 Buick?

Witness: All I got is this here. [He holds up C-1]

Me: Which we have already agreed is not a title, and doesn't have the name of anyone in your family on it, correct?

Eckert: Objection. Asked and answered.

Court: Sustained.

Me: One more thing, Mr. Harrold. Look at the bottom of C-1 and please tell the jury what state issued that form.

Witness: New York

Me: So that piece of paper that doesn't have your name on it and isn't a title, isn't even from Pennsylvania, is it?

Eckert: Objection.

Court: Sustained.

Me: No further questions.

And that was pretty much it for the testimony. Eckert called the arresting officer and his partner, but as they hadn't seen anything themselves, they didn't add much to the case. All they could say was that when they arrived, Jenkins was in the middle of removing the original fake wood steering wheel and replacing it with a chain-link one, and that one of them had taken the "title" from Jamaal Jenkins, after he offered it to the police as proof of his ownership of the Buick. The car, incidentally, had no plates, no insurance, and no inspection to go along with no title.

Both sides rested, and we went straight into closing arguments.

"Members of the jury, this has been one of the stranger car theft cases I have ever been associated with. When I tell you that it is most unusual for a car thief to demand that the owner give him the title, as well as the keys, you can trust me. Then there is the whole question of who, if anyone, owns this 1977 Buick that was the object of so much contention.

"But first, let's take a look at these charges one-by-one, and see if we can't dispose of some of the obviously defective ones. On the charge of robbery, the victim being Bruce Harrold, I think you will all agree with me that Bruce Harrold's own testimony absolutely destroyed that charge. He admitted that there was no gun and no robbery, because he lost the car in a bet with Mr. Jenkins. If there was any remaining doubt about that, then the fact that Bruce went back to his house and brought the...well, let's call it a "title" for now, because that's what the witnesses called it. Bruce Harrold brought this title to Jamaal Jenkins voluntarily, because he lost the car on a bet. So, you should not need much time to reach a "not guilty" verdict the charges relating to the robbery of Bruce Harrold. The same goes for the other charges relating to Bruce Harrold, because there was no crime, only a foolish wager.

"Now, let's look at the evidence of aggravated assault by Jamaal Jenkins against Calvin Harrold. First of all, Calvin himself was very frank with you. He told you that, in his opinion, the nameless individual with the gun was not trying to shoot him, but only to scare him. So, if you believe his testimony, and you have no reason not to, then there was no aggravated assault. Why do I say this? Because, aggravated assault, like any assault, requires the specific intent on the part of the assailant to injure another person. If the intent is anything else, like trying to scare the other person, it's not an assault.

"But, if some of you *still* aren't convinced by Calvin Harrold's testimony, I will give you another, even better reason to find my client not guilty of this charge. Here it is: there is no evidence that Jamaal Jenkins had a gun, fired any shots, or indeed did anything else that could possibly be interpreted as attempting to harm Calvin Harrold. The lone shot fired was by an unknown person about whom we know absolutely nothing. Calvin Harrold says the man was a friend of my client, but of course that is his conclusion, based solely on speculation. There is not enough evidence on this point to prove that the shooter and Mr. Jenkins even knew each other.

"The Commonwealth's theory is that Mr. Jenkins is guilty of aggravated assault because he and the anonymous gunman conspired to shoot at Calvin Harrold. But what evidence is there of a conspiracy? Did Jamaal Jenkins have any responsibility for the actions of the man with the gun? He didn't give him the gun. He didn't point out Calvin Harrold and tell him to shoot. He didn't tell or ask the other man to do anything. In fact, there is no evidence in the record of this case to indicate that Jamaal Jenkins ever said *anything* to this mysterious shooter. Mr. Eckert will undoubtedly ask you to "use your common sense," and conclude, commonsensically, that my client and the other two men were friends, and therefore must have talked to each other. All that is really more speculation than common sense. But even if you agree with this tenuous logic, that still doesn't tell you what they talked about, and as far as them agreeing to form a conspiracy, that would be guesswork piled on guesswork, without a shred of evidence. Anyway, how could they form a conspiracy against Calvin Harrold before he got to the playground? They didn't know he was coming. They didn't do it *after* he got there, that much is certain.

"So, if you base your decision on the testimony you heard from the witness stand you shouldn't have any problem deciding that the Commonwealth didn't prove Jamaal Jenkins was guilty of aggravated assault beyond a reasonable doubt. They didn't even *begin* to prove it.

"Finally, there are the charges of receiving stolen property in the form of an automobile and conspiracy to commit the same. Put aside, for the moment, the total and complete failure of the Commonwealth to show that Jamaal Jenkins was conspiring with anybody. Forget even that Bruce Harrold admitted that he lost the car to the defendant on a wager. It would still have been literally impossible for Jamaal Jenkins to steal the car.

"Why? Theft is defined in the Criminal Code as "the taking or withholding the property of another person without the owner's permission." So, in order for an act to be a theft, the property must be taken from either the owner or a person authorized by the owner to possess the property. Which brings us to the Buick. *Nobody* who testified at this trial established any ownership right in that car. Although it is true that the Harrolds and my client were laboring under the mistaken idea that this [I pick up C-1] incomplete form for the transfer of a motor vehicle title, somehow was actually a title of ownership for this car. But they were wrong: Mr.

Jenkins could not have stolen the car, nor received it as stolen property, nor conspired to do either of these things, because he did not get it from the owner. We don't know who the owner is, or if there even *is* an owner, but we do know this: nobody involved in this case has any more right to this car than I, the judge, Mr. Eckert, or you twelve jurors. To prove that Jamaal Jenkins is guilty of theft, the Commonwealth had to present evidence that the property was taken without the permission or authority of the owner. That is an element of the crime that must be *proven*: it can't just be assumed. And since nobody knows who the owner is, it is literally impossible for the Commonwealth to prove that a theft has taken place.

"To summarize, the Commonwealth has failed utterly to prove any of the charges against Jamaal Jenkins beyond a reasonable doubt, or to come anywhere near it. So, I ask you to please render your verdict accordingly: not guilty on all charges."

Eckert's case was in tatters, but you wouldn't have known it by the confident way he rose to deliver his summation. Maybe that was because he still believed he had a winner. Maybe he just didn't know the meaning of the word "quit." Perhaps he didn't know the meaning of a lot of words, such as futile, useless, and hopeless. Wisely, he recalled only the direct testimony of his witnesses to the jury, possibly in the hope that the jury would completely forget that the cross examinations had ever happened. Here is a representative sample of his argument:

"Members of the jury, despite what defense counsel has said, proof beyond a reasonable doubt is not some impossibly high standard. All you need to do is ignore distractions and irrelevant details, stay focused on the facts, and above all use your common sense. And if you do that, you will be able to see that the Commonwealth not only proved the defendant guilty beyond a reasonable doubt on all counts, but did so overwhelmingly...

"Bruce Harrold told you exactly how the defendant took his car away from him. He pointed a gun at Bruce and said, "Give me the keys. I'm taking the car." And that should appeal to your common sense, because it sounds like something that might really happen. Compare that to the story defense counsel would have you believe that he lost the car gambling on a basketball game. Would any of you do such a foolish thing with a car you had just been given by your father? No, of course not. Taking property from another person by force or the threat of force is robbery, as the judge will explain to you. And that is exactly what the defendant, Jamaal Jenkins did...

"And by taking the keys, he was also guilty of stealing the car, exactly as if he had jumped in the driver's seat, hot-wired it and drove away, because taking the keys to another person's car is, under the law, exactly the same as taking the car itself, because the thief has deprived the owner the use of the car, and has taken control of it from the owner. So, by using your common sense and applying the law that the learned judge will give you, you will be able to see that the charge of theft of a motor vehicle was also proven beyond a reasonable doubt.

"It is true that Calvin Harrold said that he didn't believe that the defendant's friend was aiming at him or trying to hit him with the shot he fired, but that does not mean that you must therefore find the defendant not guilty of this crime, as defense counsel urges. You are the sole finders of fact in this case. It is not for any witness to determine those facts, nor for counsel. So, you are free to disagree with Calvin Harrold, and follow your common sense, which tells you that nobody shoots a gun at another person unless they mean business, unless they want to put a bullet in that other person, unless they want to hurt that person, and to hurt him seriously. That is what the charge of aggravated assault means, and that is what the defendant, Jamaal Jenkins, conspired with his friends to do.

"Conspiracy, contrary to what defense counsel told you, does not require proof of a specific verbal agreement between the conspirators to commit a crime. The agreement may be shown by circumstantial evidence, by the *actions* of the conspirators, even if no words are exchanged. And that's what happened here. There was no need for Jamaal Jenkins to say anything to his friend with the gun. They both understood that Mr. Jenkins wanted the other man to use that gun, when Calvin Harrold approached the car with his baseball bat. And the law states that all conspirators to a crime are all guilty of that crime, even if one of them did not commit any overt act. So, common sense tells you that since Jamaal Jenkins' co-conspirator committed an aggravated assault, Jenkins himself is guilty as well...

"Before I conclude, I just want to say a few words about the ridiculous claim by defense counsel that there was no proof that the Harrolds were the legitimate owners of the 1977 Buick that Jamaal Jenkins took from Bruce Harrold at gunpoint, and that therefore, you cannot find his client guilty of theft or robbery. Don't allow his tricky, complicated arguments to lead you astray. As the finders of fact, I remind you again, it is solely your decision to make about the ownership of the car, just as it is with every other fact. Your common sense will tell you that whoever had the legitimate right to possess that vehicle, it certainly wasn't Jamaal Jenkins. Stealing something does not make it yours...

"Members of the jury, Jamaal Jenkins is guilty of robbery, because he pointed a gun at Bruce Harrold and took the keys to Bruce's car. He also is guilty of theft by taking, because of the same act. Jamaal Jenkins is guilty of aggravated assault, because he conspired with another man to fire a bullet at Calvin Harrold with the intent to cause serious bodily injury. The evidence of guilt is overwhelming, and I ask you to do your duty as jurors, use your common sense and find Jamaal Jenkins guilty of all charges."

Given what he had to work with, I thought it was a good effort, better than I had expected. It might even work, I thought, if the jury collectively suffered an attack of explosive amnesia that affected only their memories of the cross-examination. But then, I almost always find my own arguments irresistible, and I know that not everyone finds them as persuasive as I do.

By the time the judge finished charging the jury with the law, it was 4:30, so instead of starting deliberations so late in the day, she sent them all home with instructions to return at 9:00 sharp the next morning.

After the jurors left the courtroom, Judge Steele said, "I want both counsel to know that I thought you both gave excellent arguments...," which took me completely by surprise. As far as I could remember, she had never before complimented me on anything, not even my tie. Even more surprising, she had handed out the compliments impartially, which was completely at odds with my previous experiences in Steele's courtroom.

Then she added, "...especially *you*, Mr. Eckert." There, I thought, that's the Marjorie Steele *I* know.

I did not return to the courtroom the next day, but hung out in my downtown office, waiting for a call from the court that the jury had reached a verdict. I didn't have anything much to do there, but I saw no reason to spend any more time than was absolutely necessary in the same room as Judge Steele. Around noon, I got a call from Steele's clerk, telling me to return right away.

"They have a verdict?" I asked.

"No," he said, "just a question."

Actually, it turned out that they had two questions. They wanted to know if they could have a transcript of Calvin Harrold's testimony, and they asked if the judge could read them the definition of conspiracy again.

"Well?" Steele asked Eckert and me after she had read the jury's note to us. "I am going to grant the second request. What would you like me to do about the first one? Obviously, there's no transcript to give them..." [because the court reporter took notes in a shorthand code that was indecipherable to untrained eyes] "...but I guess the reporter could read back the testimony."

"I would have no objection to letting them hear Calvin Harrold's direct testimony," Eckert said.

How generous of him, I thought. "I don't know how you could interpret the jury's request to mean that they only wanted his *direct* testimony," I said. "It's pretty clear that they are asking to hear *all* of it. However," I added, "I can't see any reason to read all that back to them. The trial was only two days long, and unless they ask for something more specific, I would just tell them to use their memories."

It looked as if it was physically painful for her, but Judge Steele said, "I agree with Mr. Heller. This was not a long or complicated case, and they should be able to rely on their collective memory to determine the facts." She had the jury brought back into the room, did what she said she was going to do, and sent them back.

I sensed that they might be close to a verdict, so I elected to stay for a while. A half-hour later, the jury sent out another note, this one asking if Commonwealth Exhibit 1, the pink "title" could be sent back to the room. Eckert opposed granting this request, and I was in favor. Judge Steele dithered, then finally decided that the jury could look at the exhibit, but only while they were seated in the jury box under her watchful eye. Possibly she was afraid the jurors might damage or alter this wrinkled, incomplete, unsigned form issued by the New York State bureaucracy.

The jurors treated C-1 with the respect normally given to an 800-year-old illuminated manuscript, handling it with the greatest care, and taking their time examining it. Now, I was even more certain they were close to a verdict.

Forty-five minutes later, there was a heavy knock from the other side of the door to the jury deliberation room. The court officer went into the room and returned in just a few seconds to announce, "Your Honor, they have a verdict."

"Okay, bring them in," Steele said.

"All persons will rise and remain standing until the jury is seated," the court officer said.

The jurors shuffled in, carrying their handbags, newspapers, coats, and other miscellaneous possessions, and settled into their chairs. I looked at them, and a couple of them smiled back at me.

"The foreman will rise," the judge said. This was a scrawny, balding, retired postal worker from Northeast Philadelphia, a white, lower-middle-class part of the city, whose residents were not notably sympathetic to young, black criminal defendants like Jamaal Jenkins.

"Do you have a verdict as to all counts of the indictment?" Steele asked.

"Yes, we do, Your Honor," he answered.

She nodded. "Please proceed.'

The foreman looked down at the verdict sheet in his hand and read, "On count one, Robbery, we find the defendant Not Guilty. On count two, Robbery of a Motor Vehicle, we find the defendant Not Guilty. On count three, Theft of a Motor Vehicle, we find the defendant Not Guilty..."

And that was how it went, all the way to the last charge. Jamaal Jenkins patted me on the shoulder and shook my hand enthusiastically. "Thank you, Mr. Heller," he said. "I..." Then he was gaveled into silence by the judge. The crier seconded the judge by bellowing, "Quiet in the courtroom!"

I looked up at Judge Steele. Her lips were drawn in a thin white line, her forehead was deeply furrowed, her eyebrows dangerously lowered. When she spoke, she bit each word off in a way that strongly suggested that she was not at all happy.

"The court is grateful to the jury for your...*service*. You are discharged and may go," she said, not sounding especially grateful. Normally, whatever the result, the judge will give a jury his or her sincere thanks, and explain how essential they are to the functioning of the legal system. This was the shortest and least friendly jury send-off I had ever heard. Judge Steele had obviously expected a different result (although I couldn't imagine why,) and was not very successful at hiding her disappointment from the jury, who all took the hint and skedaddled.

Before the door had closed behind the final departing juror, the judge was on her feet and shouting, "I will see both counsel in my robing room, right *now*!" She marched off the bench back to her sanctum behind the bench.

I looked at the prosecutor. "*Another* fine mess you've gotten us into, Mr. Eckert," I said. He ignored my attempt to cheer him up with a little humor, and followed closely by yours truly, went back to see the judge.

Steele was pacing back and forth behind her desk when we entered. Without taking the time to offer us tea, inquire after our family's health, or even ask us to sit down, she snapped, "I want to know what just happened here."

I assumed that she was familiar enough with criminal trials that she was not asking us to explain that the jury had decided the defendant was not guilty, and the trial was over, so I was at something of a loss for what sort of answer she was looking for.

There was a palpable silence. Mr. Eckert understandably did not want the raging judge to direct her attention towards him, and wisely stood mute. For my part, I was no more eager to become the focus of Steele's wrath than was the prosecutor.

"Well, Mr. Heller?" She growled, when she tired of waiting for an answer.

"Well, Your Honor," I said, stalling while I tried to think of something that might mollify her, "*I* would say that the jury..." I hesitated. I did not want her to think that I was treating her like a simpleton, when I stated the simple and obvious truth. This judge was fully capable of hitting me with a contempt citation if she thought I was being disrespectful to her high office. (In reality, I had the greatest respect for the office, but almost none for this particular holder of it.)

I decided the best approach would be to treat her, not as if she was an idiot, but the same way I would deal with a dangerous lunatic. "Hmm...," I said, "it would appear that the jury had reasonable doubt on all the charges, Your Honor." Really, what else was there to say? (Other than to add that, in my opinion, the Commonwealth had gone to trial on one of the crappiest cases in my experience, and that if Mr. Eckert had possessed the brains of a jar of wheat germ, he would have disposed of it with a misdemeanor plea offer, or just dropped the prosecution entirely. I didn't think this would soothe Judge Steele, however, so I kept it to myself.)

She glared at me balefully, no doubt turning over ways to punish me for the offense of winning another case. (I should say here that this was my third straight win in her room.) Luckily, she couldn't think of anything, so she had to settle for an *ex post facto* threat. "Mr. Heller, if you ever try to pull your stunts in my courtroom again, I *promise* you will be sorry," she said. "Is that clear?"

Not especially, I thought. Which "stunts" was she talking about? Cross-examining witnesses? Objecting to hearsay? Getting a not guilty verdict? I decided that it was the better part of wisdom not to ask, so I just said, "Yes, Your Honor," by which I meant, "No, not at all, Your Honor."

"Good!" she declared. "Then you and your client get out of my courtroom, before I hold you both in contempt."

I didn't have to be asked twice; I made like an egg and beat it.

Afterwards, when I had time to consider the matter, I thought it was too bad that Professor Levin was longer alive, so I would never be able to tell him about the case of the car that nobody owned.

Snapshot: How I Almost Got My Own Boeing 767

One way I made a few additional bucks was to take in the occasional collection case. These would come to me at irregular intervals from a New York civil firm where I worked briefly after leaving the Kings County DA's Office. This involved a relatively simple process of domesticating the judgment in the county where the deadbeat (a technical term for "debtor") resided, having the sheriff serve notice on the debtor, then listing whatever property owned by the debtor that was readily available (real estate was best, since it was so hard to hide) for a sheriff's sale.

For some reason, debtors would often completely ignore the initial notice from the sheriff, and would not react at all until a yellow sheet of paper declaring that the premises would be sold at public auction by the sheriff on such-and-such a date, was tacked to the door of their home or business. Then they would fly into a panic, call their attorneys, who would in turn call me to ask me how I dared to sic the sheriff on the client, who was invariably an important and respected member of the community, blah, blah, blah.

Once the lawyer was satisfied that he had sufficiently defended the honor of his client, we got down to cases, which is to say, how much money it would take to settle the judgment. This amount was, by a startling string of coincidences, almost always exactly equal to the amount of the judgment. I did offer to cover the postage for the check, but that was about all the negotiating necessary, because I had a judgment, and when you have a judgment, you don't have to settle for two cents less than the full amount.

Probably the most unusual judgment I ever handled wasn't for a paying client; it was for my step-father.

Since he was an important businessman (in his own opinion, at any rate) Lou was used to having his way in business disputes. So, when he got into a tussle with British Airways over $2000 worth of frequent flier miles, and the airline representatives failed to understand who they were dealing with (i.e., an important businessman,) Lou called in the family lawyer, Yours Truly, to make them see reason.

Actually, Lou had what I considered to be a piss-poor case. He did indeed have the frequent flier miles he claimed; the only problem was that he did not get them as a passenger on British Airways. The miles had been raked up on what BA called a "partner" airline, one that provided connecting service to destinations not served by British Airways. In this instance, the partner was the Dutch national airline, KLM. Lou wanted to buy a ticket on British Airways with his KLM miles, and British Airways was not going to accept the KLM miles.

Still, as a dutiful step-son (not to mention the fact that the man had very generously paid my way through Villanova Law School, a matter of many thousands of dollars,) I filed an action against

British Airways in small-claims court, asking for $2000. Then I went over to the counter maintained by the airline in an office building in Center City Philadelphia, where I served a copy of the Summons and Complaint on the British Airways representative working there. When the court date duly arrived, I still had heard nothing from the defendant, so I moseyed over to the small claims court to take a default judgment. I had won! Hurray!

Now it was time to execute the judgment. The only property British Airways had in Center City was the tiny counter where I had served the summons and complaint. I did not see how a sheriff's auction could raise $2000 from selling anything there.

So, I made a couple of phone calls, then took my judgment down to the sheriff's office in City Hall. I stepped up to the counter and told the clerk, "I want to enforce a judgment against the assets of an airline, so I need the notice to be posted down at the airport."

The clerk looked over my judgment, then pulled out a map of Philadelphia. "Part of the airport is in Delaware County and part of it is in Philadelphia. Let me see if I can figure out which county British Airways is in."

After devoting several minutes to his map, he excused himself to make a phone call. When he returned, the clerk said, "As near as I can tell, their counter inside the terminal is in Delaware County, but the planes actually operate from the Philadelphia part of the airport."

"Excellent," I said. "I want your man to post the notice of judgment and sheriff's sale on one of their planes when it docks at the terminal."

"Fine," he said. "Just put that in the special instructions section at the bottom here." He shoved a form over to me. I filled it out, paid the sheriff's fee (the costs for collection are added to the judgment and paid by the debtor, naturally), and walked away, whistling cheerily.

Two days later, the phone in my office rang. I picked up the phone and said, "Law Office, Andrew Heller speaking. How can I help you?"

"How can you *help* me?" He repeated, in tones of hysteria, bordering on panic. "You can call off your dogs, that's how. Do you know that somebody from the Philadelphia Sheriff's Department just posted a notice on the door of one of our 767s and they're going to seize it to pay off a judgment against us? Did you *know* that?"

Although the caller had identified neither himself nor the entity he represented, I had no trouble deducing the nature of his errand. "There, there, my good man," I said in my most soothing voice. "I'm sure it's not as bad as all that. Now, why don't you tell me who you are, then *slowly* explain what you're calling me about."

The caller pulled himself together enough to give me his name and his position with British Airways. He explained the disastrous consequences that would ensue if one of their $150 million airplanes was seized and sold at a sheriff's sale. He implored me to tell him how to make this problem go away.

"It's simple," I told him. "Just get a check for $2000 plus costs to me, and as soon as it's on my desk, I will call up the sheriff and tell him the judgment is satisfied. Tomorrow, I'll file a notice of settlement in small claims court, and that'll be the end of it."

"We'll have the check ready in ten minutes, and I'll have it sent from out Center City to you by messenger. You should have it in less than a half-hour."

He was as good as his word; better even. The messenger knocked on my door 25 minutes after I hung up the phone, to deliver a check in the amount of $2,250. I did what I promised, although I could not help feeling a little regret for settling so easily when I had a chance to own a personal 216-seat Boeing 767-100 airliner.

But when I thought it over, I decided that my life was already too complicated without adding the parking, upkeep, crew salaries and all the rest that went with the ownership of multi-million-dollar airplane.

Snapshot: Renting from Chompy and Other Juvenile Pranks

Another way to supplement my meager income was to take appointments to represent juvenile defendants in delinquency court. Juvenile defendants can be charged with same offenses as adults, are entitled to a free court-appointed attorney if they cannot afford one, and have the same right to a trial (called, in juvenile court, an "adjudicatory hearing,") except that they do not have the right to have their case heard by a jury of their peers (who presumably would also be juveniles).

The main difference was that a juvenile was not found "guilty" or "not guilty," but was either "delinquent" or not. If the former, the juvenile defendant did not receive a sentence, like an adult. Instead, the court would decide whether the delinquent was "in need of treatment, supervision, or rehabilitation." This could range from being placed on probation and returned to his home (if he had one,) to placement in one of the high-security juvenile facilities that are prisons in all but name. Incidentally, many of these juvenile prisons used by the Pennsylvania courts are operated by private companies, and located all over the United States, so that a Pennsylvania delinquent offender may end up spending years in a concrete cell in Texas, Florida or some other place far from their family, friends, and most important, the supervision of the court. In addition, a judge can keep a juvenile offender under his control until age 21. The courts are not required to state a definite term of incarceration; they can hold a juvenile as long as, in the judge's opinion, the delinquent is in need of treatment, supervision, or rehabilitation.

Since they were presumably acting in the best interests of the child, juvenile court judges are given leave by the higher courts to be even more arbitrary in their conduct of trials than their adult court colleagues. A juvenile court judge will have to really screw up a trial before the Superior Court will take an appeal from a delinquency adjudication seriously. After all, the defendants haven't been convicted of a crime, only adjudicated, they aren't incarcerated, only placed under supervision, and most of the time, the juvenile records are expunged when the individual reaches adulthood. So, it seems reasonable (to the appellate courts, anyway) to relax the legal standards for these cases, informally, if not officially.

Attorneys are paid less for juvenile appointments than for adult cases, but you could get a lot of them, and if you could schedule them right, they could give you some paying work on slow days, when you had nothing going on in Common Pleas. Juvenile clients were generally just minor-league versions of adult clients, except that the former were even worse at creating justifications or explanations for their crimes. Some of them were so unsophisticated that they would even tell me the truth.

For example, I was appointed to represent a 13-year-old charged with aggravated assault on a classmate after school. He told me that he and his friends were walking down the street, minding their own business, when they saw the complainant across the street. My client said that the other boy challenged him and his gang to a fight, which I found a little hard to believe, as he was alone, and my client had several friends with him. Naturally, my client could not let this challenge go unanswered, especially since it came from a cowardly weakling (he didn't bother to hide his contempt for the victim,) so he and his little gang crossed over the street, surrounded the other kid, and beat the living crap out of him. I think the complaining witness lost a few teeth and had a hairline fracture in one orbital socket of his left eye.

"Uh-huh," I said after hearing this…I guess I'd call it his "defense." "So how did he challenge you to fight? Did he say something?"

"Nah," my client answered, "he didn't say nothing."

"Well, how did you know he wanted to fight you, then?" I asked.

"Oh," the client shrugged, "he was *lookin'* at me."

I did not understand this at all. Maybe, I thought, *"lookin'"* was street lingo for something other than "looking."

"He was *looking* at you?" I asked. "With his eyes, is that what you mean?"

"Yeah, you know, lookin'," he repeated.

"So, you knew he wanted to fight all four of you, because he looked at you?" I asked, just to make absolutely sure I wasn't missing something.

"Yeah, that's right, Mr. Heller," he said, clearly relieved that his slow-witted lawyer finally understood what he was saying. "You got it."

He was adjudicated delinquent, found to be in need of treatment, supervision, or rehabilitation (which was, in my opinion, a considerable understatement,) and packed off to Hat and Boot camp, a kind of Parris Island for delinquents. What happened to him in later life, I cannot say, but he had already made significant progress towards a career as an enforcer for a drug dealer or collector for a loan shark.

One of the most common crimes in juvenile court was car theft. There are certain models that are remarkably easy to start without a key, by simply breaking open the ignition collar, inserting a screwdriver and wrapping a couple of wires around the shaft. Since juvenile car thieves usually had no idea of how to sell the car to a chop shop, they would drive it around for a while, then sell it for a few dollars to whoever happened to be around when they got tired of the car (unless they had already cracked up the car, which happened quite frequently, since 12-, 13- and 14-year-old thieves were not, on the whole, very good drivers.)

My client in this particular case insisted that when the police stopped him, he was legitimately in possession of the car, a late-model Acura, as he had rented it for $5 from a man in his neighborhood.

I didn't even bother to ask if the screwdriver in the ignition didn't make him suspicious. Instead, I doggedly pursued the details of this unusual rental agreement.

"So, who was this man you rented the car from?" I asked.

"He's just some old wino who hangs around the 'hood, you know," he said.

Ah-ha, I thought. A derelict wino who owns a $10,000 car and rents it out to adolescent kids for $5. Sounds reasonable.

"Well, how well do you know this guy?" I asked.

"Oh, I know him real good," the client assured me. "I see him all the time."

"Good," I said. "Maybe we can subpoena him and have him testify for you. What's his name?"

"Chompy," the client answered. "That's what everybody calls him, 'cause his teeth is all messed up." He opened his mouth and pointed to several places where Chompy was suffering from dental deficits.

"Right, but that's not his real name," I said.

"All I know him by is Chompy," the client insisted.

"Well, tell me where he lives then," I said.

"I don't know," the client answered.

"So, what *do* you know about him, other than that he's a wino, and people call him Chompy?" I asked.

He thought about this for a few seconds, then said, "Nothin' much, I guess."

"But you said you *know* him," I insisted, knowing full well I was wasting time trying to get any useful information from this source.

"Oh, yeah, I *know* him, all right," the client said. "I just don't know him like *that*."

Ten: The Short Ones Are Always the Troublemakers

As I said at the beginning, the trials in this book were not very important, except to the people directly involved. To the defendants, the outcome of the case was usually very important, and sometimes overwhelmingly so. The below case is an exception: it held no greater importance for the defendant than it did for the rest of the universe, which is to say, roughly none. Yet, it did have some interesting, and even instructive, features.

Skeeter Johnson was a not a big man, nor even an average-sized one. It would be more accurate to describe him as a runt. He was 5'4", and a scrawny, unhealthy-looking 110 pounds dripping wet. But it would be a mistake to conclude from his physical dimensions that he was not dangerous, because he was. He had recently been convicted of attempted murder and aggravated assault, and picked up a new arrest while he was sitting in the county jail awaiting sentencing on the conviction. By the time the new case (to which I had been appointed) got to trial, he had already been sentenced to ten to twenty years on the first case.

The new charge was aggravated assault as a felony of the 2nd degree. It was really a jumped-up misdemeanor simple assault (knowingly causing bodily injury to another person) that becomes a felony when the victim is any one of a number of designated public officials, including cops, firemen, judges, state liquor store employees, probation officers, and another thirty or so other categories, including the one relevant to this case, prison guards. He was charged with breaking the hand of a guard while he was lodged at the Detention Center after his conviction awaiting his sentencing date.

When I got to the courtroom, I was pleased to discover that I was up against my old friendly enemy, Jan McAfee, again. The luck of the draw pitted us against each other more often than the laws of chance would have predicted. I think I had seven or eight trials against her, and won about half of them. She was a good, smart attorney, who always fought hard, but clean, and never tried to use underhanded tricks, like enlisting the judge's help against the defense.

The judge, the Honorable Bernie Willis, and a decent enough sort, called us back to his robing room to see if he could get us to settle this case with a plea deal, rather going to the time and trouble of a jury trial (naturally, I preferred a jury to a bench trial before any judge in the entire First Judicial District.)

"Ms. McAfee," he said, "I will tell you right now that in the event this defendant is convicted by the jury, I have no intention of imposing even one day of consecutive time. He will either be acquitted, or sentenced to concurrent time, so I can't see any reason for the District Attorney not to offer him a concurrent sentence in the first place, like 2 to 4 years on the F-2 aggravated assault."

He turned to me. "Mr. Heller, if the Commonwealth does make the kind of offer I am suggesting, I would hope that you would strongly recommend to your client that he accept. There is absolutely nothing to gain for him here."

Jan McAfee was no dummy, as I have said, and she was way ahead of the judge. "Your Honor, I tendered an offer of 1 ½ to 3 years concurrent to Mr. Heller, as soon as I learned he had been appointed." She and the judge both looked at me expectantly.

"That is correct, Your Honor," I said. "And when I visited Mr. Johnson last week, I advised him to take it, for essentially the same reasons you just stated. Unfortunately, I am going to have to disappoint you, Judge. My client not only rejected the Commonwealth's offer, he was very emphatic about it. Mr. Johnson feels that that *he* was the victim in this case, and that he would not plead guilty if, here I am paraphrasing, the Commonwealth offered to let him plead guilty to holding an overdue library book."

"So, I take it that you do not see any realistic possibility of a non-trial disposition here, Mr. Heller," the judge said.

"That's about the size of it, Your Honor," I agreed.

"Can you at least advise him to waive the jury trial?" Judge Willis asked.

I did my best to look regretful. "I discussed this issue with him at length, and Mr. Johnson said he wanted a *jury* to hear what they had done to him," I explained. "He does not trust judges. Maybe it has something to do with the 10-to-20 he caught for his attempted murder case." When Jan and Judge Willis looked puzzled, I added, "That was a waiver trial."

"Ah, I see," the judge said, nodding.

I did not see fit to say that I had urged Mr. Johnson to take a jury, because as conflict counsel, I was getting paid by the day, and the longer the trial, the more money I made. I hasten to add that I truly believe that a jury trial is *always* better for the defendant than a bench trial. The only reason a lawyer should advise the client to waive his right to a jury trial is if the lawyer knows his skills are insufficient for a jury trial.

We went back out to the courtroom, one of the judge's minions called downstairs to order a panel, and we spent the rest of the morning and all the afternoon picking our jury. We ended up with what I thought was an unusually educated group. I can remember a professor from the University of Pennsylvania, a civil engineer, a writer, a teacher from an upscale private school, and I think that all or almost all of the others had earned at least a bachelor's degree. It is not true that possession of a college degree is an unfailing indicator of bleeding-heart liberalism, but I believed that I was more effective with well-educated jurors, because my arguments generally appealed to the minds of the jury, and rarely to their emotions. I wasn't very good at the latter, as I had discovered whenever I tried it in the past.

We started the trial the following morning. Jan McAfee's opening was as always, succinct and professional. It was even more succinct than usual, because the facts in this case were so simple and she only had one witness, the correctional officer.

My opening was even shorter. I just thanked the jury for coming to our little party, reminded them that Mr. Johnson, as he sat before their judgment, was innocent, and that he would remain in that state of grace, unless the Commonwealth proved his guilt beyond a reasonable doubt. I added a few more generalities, and urged them to consider all the evidence and the arguments of both sides before coming to any conclusion, then sat down to watch Jan McAfee open the bidding by calling C.O. Albert Kowalska to the stand. Kowalska was a large, muscular individual, who looked like he had been an offensive lineman at some point in his life. He had had a friendly, honest-looking face, the kind that jurors tend to trust, which I didn't care for at all. His (slightly edited) direct testimony went as follows:

McAfee: Good morning, Officer Kowalska.

Witness: Good morning, Counselor.

McAfee: Officer Kowalska, how are you employed?

Witness: I am a prison guard for the Philadelphia Department of Corrections.

McAfee: How long have you been so employed?

Witness: 16 years.

McAfee: Were you working on July 16 of 2003?

Witness: Yes. I was working at the Detention Center that day.

McAfee: What were your duties that day?

Witness: Officer John Neill and I were transferring inmates to new cells, to allow cleaning crews to go in and clean up the cells. It's routinely done once a week.

McAfee: Did anything unusual happen on that day that brings you to court today?

Witness: Yes. When we reached Mr. Johnson's cell...

McAfee: Would that be the defendant, Edward Johnson?

Witness: Yes. When I opened his cell, he was sitting on his bunk. I said, "Come on, Skeeter, get up. We have to move you across the corridor so they can clean your cell."

McAfee: By "Skeeter," are you still referring to the defendant, Edward Johnson?

Witness: Yes, ma'am. That's what everybody at the DC called him.

McAfee: When you told him to get up, how did the defendant respond?

Witness: Well, he didn't get up. He was reading a magazine when I came in, and after I told him we were moving him, he just kept on reading. He didn't even look up. He completely ignored me.

McAfee; What did you do then?

Witness: I went over to him, put my hand on the magazine, and said, "Come on, Skeeter. I don't have time to fool with you today. Get up."

McAfee: So, did he get up?

Witness: No, ma'am. He snatched the magazine away from me, and started reading again.

McAfee: What happened next?

Witness: I said, "Come on, let's *go*!", ripped the magazine out of his hands, and threw it on the floor.

McAfee: What did the defendant do when you took his magazine.

Witness: He hauled off and hit me.

McAfee: He struck you with his fist?

Witness: Correct. He hit me on my left arm, right about here.

McAfee: For the record, the witness is indicating a place on his left biceps about midway between the shoulder and elbow. What did you do then, Officer Kowalska?

Witness: I hit him back. I punched him in the head.

McAfee: What part of the defendant's head did you hit?

Witness: On the left side, around here.

McAfee: For the record, indicating an area just above the left temple. What effect did your blow have on Mr. Johnson?

Witness: It knocked him over on his side. I waited until he sat up, and said, "Are you coming now?" This time, he got up and let us take him over to the other cell without making any more trouble.

McAfee: Did you suffer any injuries as a result of this incident?

Witness: My right hand was sore after I hit Johnson, but I didn't think much of it, until after Neill and I finished moving the prisoners. Then I noticed it was still sore, and it had swollen up.

McAfee: Did you seek medical attention at that time?

Witness: Not right away. First, I tried putting a bag of ice on it for a few minutes, but when that didn't help, I went down to the infirmary, where they took an x-ray.

McAfee: Did you ever learn the results of the x-ray?

Witness: Yes. The doctor told me I had a broken bone in my right hand. He sent me to Frankford Hospital to get treatment.

[I had a copy of the x-ray report and hospital records in my file, and had already agreed with Ms. McAfee to stipulate to its admission, so I did not object here.]

McAfee: What did they do for you at the hospital?

Witness: They put a splint on it, and gave me a note saying that I needed to take a week off from work to allow the bone to heal.

McAfee: What happened after that?

Witness: I returned to the Detention Center, I told my supervisor what had happened at the hospital and gave him the note from the doctor. He told me to write an incident report describing how I was injured, which I did. Then my supervisor told me that the warden wanted to see me, so I went up to his office.

McAfee: What happened at that meeting?

Witness: The warden asked me if I had reported the incident with Johnson to the police, and when I said "No," he ordered me to report it.

McAfee: And did you report it?

Witness: Yes.

McAfee: What did you report to the police?

Witness: Basically, the same thing I said here in court.

McAfee: No more questions.

I thought I detected a little embarrassment in Kowalska's voice during his last few answers, so I decided to start my cross examination by exploring this area.

Me: Officer, you said that you did not report the incident to the police until the warden ordered you report it, correct?

Witness: Correct.

Me: And if you hadn't been ordered to do it, you would never have reported it to the police, correct?

Witness: I wouldn't have reported it on my own, no.

Me: Even after you learned that you had broken a bone in your hand, you still didn't want to report it to the police.

Witness: That is correct.

I now did something a lawyer is *never* supposed to do on cross; I asked a "why' question. In cross-examination, when an attorney is trying to wring answers from a hostile witness, the last thing you want to do is ask a witness *why* he did something, and give him a chance to make his testimony look better, by explaining his reasoning.

But this time, it seemed like a good idea. C.O. Kowalska struck me as being a straightforward kind of guy. I could not detect any sign of deception in his face or voice. But I definitely did get the feeling that he really didn't want to be here, testifying in this case.

Me: Officer Kowalska, why didn't you want to report the incident when you broke your hand to the police?

Witness: Well, you know, I just didn't think it needed to go any further, that's all. Skeeter hit me, I popped him, and it was over. He acted like a jerk, and he took his lumps, and I figured that was that.

Me: You didn't feel that Mr. Johnson deserved any additional punishment, is that it?

Witness: Yes, that's pretty much it.

Me: Did you sustain any injury when Mr. Johnson hit you?

Witness: No.

After that helpful exchange I moved on.

Me: Officer Kowalska, what is your approximate height and weight?

Witness: I'm 6'4" and I weigh about 285.

Me: You were roughly the same size on July 16, 2003, correct?

Witness: Yes.

Me: Could you please stand up and turn to face the jury?

Witness stands and turns toward the jury. Standing in the witness box, three feet above the floor, he looked perfectly enormous.

Me: Thank you, Officer. You can sit down again.

Witness sits back in his chair.

Me: Officer, did you accidentally hit anything but Mr. Johnson when punched him, like a wall, for example.

Witness: No, I didn't hit a wall. The only thing I hit was his head.

Me: And you hit Mr. Johnson's head so hard that the impact fractured a bone in your hand, correct?

Witness: Yes.

I paused, trying to decide if I needed to ask anything else, then decided that this witness had given us as much help as he could. "No more questions," I said.

After Ms. McAfee moved the hospital records into evidence, we took a break for lunch. When we returned from lunch, it was time for closing arguments. Normally, as I have said, I don't even try to win jurors over with emotional appeals, because I'm not very good at that sort of argument. Anyway, I had a decent, reasonably logical argument to make in this case, on the issue of bodily injury.

The elements of simple assault are: (1) intent to cause bodily injury, and (2) causing it. True, Kowalska did suffer a broken bone in his hand, which definitely *was* bodily injury, but since he sustained the injury by slamming his fist into Johnson's skull, it wasn't easy to see how that injury could be attributed to an intentional act by the defendant.

Of course, McAfee could argue that Johnson's punch was enough show intent to cause an injury, and that he had thus committed *attempted* aggravated assault. But whether the jury could infer that particular intent from one rather weak punch was far from certain. Maybe Skeeter wasn't trying to hurt Kowalska, but just wanted him to go away, so he could read his magazine in peace. That argument might appeal to the jury.

But I was in a strange, reckless mood, and I really didn't feel like being logical. This case was almost unique, in that it meant almost nothing to the Commonwealth, the court, the public, or even to the client. After this trial was over, he was off to serve his 10-to-20 upstate, and whatever the outcome here, that would not change. So, I was free to do pretty much do as I pleased, and nobody would be the worse for it. I felt like having some fun and letting off some steam with an old-fashioned hellfire and damnation oration, so that's what I gave them.

"Members of the jury, you have heard that my client, Mr. Johnson, was in jail when he was charged with assaulting C.O. Kowalska. *Why* he was there is not relevant to this case, but I would ask you to consider that people may be incarcerated for any number of reasons, and not necessarily because they have committed a crime. So, I will ask you not to hold that against him, or to consider it as any evidence of his guilt I this case.

"But I *would* like you to think about our prison system. What is the purpose of imprisonment? There are a number of legitimate reasons: to protect society from dangerous individuals, to punish criminals, to deter others from committing crimes, and many other reasons. The punishment is the loss of the prisoner's liberty. At least, that is *supposed* to be the punishment. It is not intended to take away an individual's humanity.

"Now consider what happened here. It is true that Mr. Johnson wasn't cooperating with the guards, when the two correctional officers came to take him out of his cell. He resisted them, passively at first, and then with one feeble punch on the arm.

"In return, Kowalska, a huge, powerful man, who is 6 foot 4 and weighs 285 pounds, hit Mr. Johnson, who is 5'4" and 110, punched him in the head, hit him so hard that he broke *his own hand*! Is this any way to treat a human being? If Mr. Johnson had been a *dog*, the law would have protected him from this kind of mistreatment. Doesn't a man, a *human being* deserve as much consideration as an *animal*? Apparently not, because Kowalska wasn't charged with any offense.

"But it wasn't enough that Mr. Johnson was beaten into submission: they decided to charge *him* with a crime, when the truth is that *he* was the real victim. And that, members of the jury, is not right. If you want to live in a society where basic human rights, even those of prisoners, are acknowledged, in a country where all men can expect to be treated at least as well as dogs, you can say so, here, today, with your verdict. Let the Commonwealth know that you are outraged by this case, that such inhumane treatment of your fellow man is unacceptable, by finding the defendant, Edward Johnson, not guilty."

I had really worked myself up into a frenzy during this speech, and when I sat down, my forehead was streaming, and my face felt flushed. Jan McAfee was staring at me as if I had lost my mind. I smiled back at her, leaned closer to her table, and whispered, "So, how'd you like it?"

She rolled her eyes in answer, then got up to deliver her own, rational, closing argument.

"This is actually a very simple case. When the defendant hit Officer Kowalska with his fist, he committed the crime of simple assault, or at least attempted to commit it. Under the law, certain persons, such as judges, schoolteachers, prosecutors and correctional officers have been given special protection, so that a simple assault on a person in one of these categories automatically becomes an aggravated assault. And that's what happened here...

"The fact that Kowalska broke his hand on the defendant's skull does not change the facts, nor does it lessen the defendant's guilt in any way, shape, or form. Whether Kowalska wanted to report the crime or didn't, or if he thought Johnson should be prosecuted, are not relevant to your verdict, and you should not allow these irrelevancies to distract you...

"Your only duty here is to decide if the Commonwealth has proved the defendant guilty of aggravated assault beyond a reasonable doubt. Despite Mr. Heller's arguments, you are not here to send a message to the Commonwealth of Pennsylvania, advance the cause of prison reform, or whatever it was Mr. Heller said. You are here to decide is if the defendant is guilty of the crime charged, based on the evidence---and that is all. If you do that, you will only be able to reach one verdict: guilty as charged."

The judge read the jury their instructions on the law, and as there was only one charge, that didn't take very long. So, by 3:00 the jury had retired to deliberate.

Jan McAfee came over to me and said, "What the hell were you doing?" She demanded. "All that crap about the human rights is not going to turn your client---who's a pretty nasty piece of business, by the way---into Mahatma Gandhi. The jury's not going to buy it, especially this one. There are too many intelligent people on it."

"What can I say?" I asked. "It felt like the thing to do at the time."

The judge didn't comment directly on my argument, but when he said, "I don't think it will take them very long," I could almost hear the rest of the sentence "...to find your client guilty."

Well, the judge was right, at least about how long it took to reach a verdict. Literally fifteen minutes later, barely enough time to pick a foreperson, we heard a knock on the jury room door. A court officer went over to see what they wanted, then returned to announced, "They have a verdict, Your Honor."

The judge looked up at the clock. "Already?" He asked. "All right, bring them in."

After everyone was in his or her proper place, the judge asked the foreman (who turned out to be the professor from Penn) if the jurors were all in agreement, and when he was assured that they were, he asked the foreman to read the verdict.

"We find the defendant, Edward Johnson, Not Guilty," he said.

The judge was obviously surprised, but unlike Judge Steele, he did not take the verdict personally.

He graciously thanked the jurors for their service, praised them for performing their civic duty, and generally told them how great they were, before he let them go.

After she got over her initial shock at the verdict, Jan McAfee was a pretty good sport about it. "Nice win, Mr. Heller, not that it'll do Skeeter any good."

This was true. This verdict would have no effect on the 10-to-20 years he was about to start serving upstate. The outcome was of no consequence whatsoever to the public at large, the Commonwealth, or Johnson himself.

"Thanks, Jan." I said. "You're right, of course. Skeeter will be out of circulation for the next 10-to-20, and I can't say the thought makes me very sad."

Flush with victory (a meaningless one, perhaps, but still a victory,) I headed for home. To my surprise, half a dozen jurors were waiting for me in the hallway outside the courtroom. What could they possibly want?

"Mr. Heller," the private school teacher said, "we all think it was a *terrible* shame."

"What's that?" I asked.

"Why, what they did to your poor client," another juror answered.

"Ah, yes, I suppose it was," I agreed. Under my breath, I added, "but not *that* much of a shame."

The foreman asked, "Will you be representing him when he sues the City of Philadelphia?"

There was no possibility of such a suit, but he obviously assumed that there would be one. Rather than disillusion him, I answered, "No, I don't do civil work."

The other jurors expressed similar sentiments. A couple of them even congratulated me for the way I stood up for human rights. I was completely taken aback by the effect my amateur theatrics had on the jury. They had *believed* me when I told them that they were striking a blow for human rights by acquitting Skeeter Johnson. They were decent people, and they deserved a worthier recipient of their generous humanity.

Snapshot: Family Matters

From time to time, it's handy to have a lawyer in the family, if only to save money on legal fees. One example is the Case of the Non-Expiring Gift Certificate, or alternatively, the Great Potato Salad Caper.

It all started when a family member gave my wife, who I shall refer to, at her request, as "Esmerelda," a $35 gift certificate for a vendor at the local farmer's market. There was a date on the certificate. Presumably this was the expiration date, although this was not explicitly stated. It did not say what the date meant, not "valid until," not "Expires on....," or anything else.

The gift certificate got buried under other papers, and did not surface again until after the putative expiration date. Esmerelda thought it would be worthwhile to try to use it anyway. She went to the stall in the farmer's market, and asked the vendor for a few items that were in the refrigerated case which the vendor then placed on the counter. Then she handed the vendor the gift certificate (along with the cash register receipt from the gift certificate.) Unfortunately, the vendor steadfastly insisted that the gift certificate was expired.

Most people probably would have walked away muttering to themselves at this point. A few might have gone home to write an angry letter to the local paper, the managing company of the farmer's market, or a nasty Google review. Maybe one or two particularly litigious souls would have brought a suit against the vendor in small claims court.

Esmerelda, however, has her own, unique way of dealing with unreasonable people. She snatched a quart of potato salad from the counter, and ran for the exit. The vendor yelled for her to stop, then came out to give chase. By the time the vendor made it to the parking lot, "Esmerelda" was already pulling away in her car.

But she was not quick enough to keep the vendor from seeing and recording her license plate number. She called the local police, who ran the plate and appeared at the door of our house no more than ten minutes after the getaway. Esmerelda had not yet returned home, and the only one home to answer the door was our 13-year-old daughter.

The cop didn't believe my daughter when she said that she did not know where her mother was, and was threatening to arrest her, when Esmerelda appeared. Fortunately, she wasn't taken into custody, but the cop did give her a summons to appear before the local magistrate, on a charge of retail theft.

Two weeks later, I entered my appearance on behalf of my wife in Magisterial District Court, Justice Albert Galloway, presiding.

The case was presented by the arresting officer. (An assistant district attorney appears in magistrate courts for preliminary hearings only on felony charges and misdemeanor trials. The local cops are responsible for the prosecution of summary offenses, like retail theft). This was the same cop who had tried to bully my daughter on the day of the "crime."

She put the vendor on the stand. The vendor told the judge, in an increasingly outraged tone, how the defendant had first asked the prices of various food items for sale and then tried to use an expired gift certificate for $35, then stole a quart of potato salad.

My cross examination went as follows:

Me: (handing the gift certificate to the shop owner) Ma'am, look at that gift certificate. Do the words "expiration date" appear anywhere on it, on either side?

Witness: It has a date written right here. It says...

Me: No. Please listen to the question: Are the words "expiration date" written on it anywhere.

Witness: No, but...

Me: Please don't answer before I ask a question. Now, the gift certificate was purchased with normal money, correct?

Witness: What do you mean?

Me: I mean that it was purchased with genuine United States currency.

Witness: Yes.

Me: And that money never expired, did it?

Witness: What does that mean?

Me: You kept the money, but you didn't have to give anything in exchange for it, did you?

Witness: Yes.

Me: You were getting $35 for nothing, weren't you?

Witness: no answer

Me: And since that time, has the value of the dollar increased or decreased? (We were in an inflationary period, so of course the $35 was worth more when the gift certificate was purchased than it was worth the day of the caper.)

Witness: I don't know. Decreased?

Me: Nothing further

I could see the judge was not going along with the notion that it was okay to use an "expired" certificate, and that was pretty much my defense. I sat down next to "Esmerelda" and said, "It doesn't look good. You want to testify?"

"You *bet* I do," she answered fiercely.

"Okay," I said. I stood up. "The defense calls Esmerelda Heller."

Me: Did you take the potato salad from that woman's stand at the farmer's market, as she testified?

Witness: Yes.

Me: Why?

Witness: That gift certificate is worth $35.

Judge: But the gift certificate expired after a year. It was no good any more.

Witness: That isn't true. It does not have any expiration date. There's a date on it, but it doesn't say what that date signifies. That could have been the date the gift certificate was purchased. I don't know. Anyway, she still has the money, so I had the right to buy something with that gift certificate.

Judge: You *still* don't understand, do you? Once I had a gift certificate for a baseball glove, but it expired and I could not use it anymore. Do you really not understand how gift certificates work? They expire.

Witness: It does not have any expiration date.

Judge: (Shaking his head, and staring at the witness in disbelief.) You are a seriously confused young woman. You clearly don't understand the nature of your actions here. I don't have any choice... I have to find you not guilty.

Although he did not use the term, the judge's ruling was based on a legal concept called "diminished capacity." It is related to an insanity defense, but a lesser standard, when the defendant's condition does not quite meet one of the legal definitions of insanity, such as: "being unable to distinguish between right and wrong," "unable to understand the nature and quality of his actions," "unable to control his actions," and so on. Diminished capacity refers to the defendant's mental inability to form the intent necessary to commit a particular crime (see Pancakes & Syrup, above.)

As I explained to Esmerelda afterwards, basically, the magistrate had found her to be too loony to understand that she had broken the law, so he was obliged to let her off. She spent the entire ride home fuming that she wasn't loony, although she was at least satisfied with the outcome of the trial.

Of course, we can never go back to that farmer's market again.

[Note: The above account was primarily written by my wife, who had a much better memory of the details of her brush with the law. A.H.]

That was not the only time I had to defend my wife in court. There was also the incident where she got a traffic ticket for running a stop sign in the parking lot of a local shopping center. Luckily for her, I had a copy of the Pennsylvania Vehicle and Traffic Law (VTL) handy, so I was able to look up law, something the cop who had issued the moving violation had not troubled himself to do. Had he done so, he would have discovered that only traffic signs on public streets and highways ("roadways" to use the official terminology) have the force of the law behind them. Stop signs and the like on private property, like the parking lots of shopping centers, are advisory in nature, and not subject to the Vehicle and Traffic Law.

I called the police precinct to explain to the cop that he had made a mistake, so he would have a chance to correct it (and incidentally, save me a trip down to Traffic Court.) But it turned out that moving violations are like the laws of the Persians and the Medes: they can never be withdrawn or changed. So, we had to go down to Center City to fight the ticket, after all.

It wasn't much of a fight. I started reading the relevant section of the VTL, and before I could finish, the judge cut it with, "Not Guilty." Another glorious victory for Rumpole!

Commentary: Innocent Until Proven Guilty and Other Myths

As I am write this book, Donald Trump's indictment for falsifying various business records was announced. Naturally, the cable news networks pulled out all stops in their coverage, bringing in not just the usual retired Federal and state prosecutors, but reinforcing them with new legal talking heads. On the network I happened to be watching, one of latter, a former assistant in the Manhattan District Attorney's office, prefaced her analysis with this completely incorrect statement of the law: "Of course, he [Trump] is innocent until proven guilty…" I could excuse a layman for saying something like that, but not a career prosecutor.

What am I talking about? Everybody knows that a defendant is innocent until proven guilty. That's the American way…isn't it?

No. In reality, there is only one stage in a criminal prosecution when a defendant is considered innocent until proven guilty: at trial. Let's just take a look at the stages of a typical criminal case, and when and if a defendant is treated as innocent.

Most felony cases begin with an arrest. (Much less often they begin with an indictment by a grand jury, but we'll skip that for now.) In theory, a person cannot be arrested and charged unless the police have probable cause to believe that he has committed a crime. Can that be squared with the assumption that this same individual is innocent until proven guilty? No, of course not. The police are not supposed to arrest *innocent* people. They are only supposed to arrest ones who are suspected of committing a crime.

So, at the very beginning, the defendant is handcuffed, locked up, fingerprinted and arraigned on a criminal charge. It is inconceivable that could be done to an innocent person. But the arrest is just the first step. Next, a court must decide whether this "innocent" individual should be released on bail, and if so, how much money he must put up to secure his release, and what additional restrictions should be imposed on him, if he is granted pre-trial release.

On the most serious charges, such as homicide, a court may decide that the suspect is not entitled to bail, and must remain incarcerated until his trial. If bail is set, but if the defendant can't raise the necessary cash, he will likewise remain locked up until trial, which may take months or even years. You may already be getting tired of reading this, but I must reiterate that this is no way to treat a presumably innocent person.

Interestingly enough, among the factors considered in setting bail, other than flight risk, are danger to the community and the likelihood of conviction. The former asks the judge to consider whether that this *innocent* person, who has not yet been found guilty of anything, should be kept in jail because of the potential danger he poses to the public. The latter allows the court to set or deny bail based on the nature of the charges and the strength of the prosecution case, at a stage when none of the allegations against the defendant have been tested, and without regard to any possible defenses to the charges, without questioning the reliability of the state's evidence, and so forth.

If a defendant were truly considered to be innocent until proven guilty, then no one would ever be held in custody pending trial. In fact, they would not even be subject to pre-trial restrictions, like ankle monitors. After all, *you* are innocent, and the government is not allowed to restrict *your* movements, so by the same token, it should not be able to infringe upon the liberty of a criminal suspect---*if,* that is, a suspect is truly innocent until proven guilty.

The next step after arraignment is either a presentation to a grand jury (in New York) or a preliminary hearing (in Pennsylvania). Both of these procedures have the same purpose: to force the state show that it has a *prima fascia* case, in other words, that the defendant probably committed the offense he is charged with. Does it make the tiniest bit of sense to apply the word "innocent" to someone who has just been indicted by a grand jury? If it does, then the word has lost all meaning.

The concept of innocence until proven guilty is generally not even given lip service outside the court system. Media outlets freely report all sorts of lurid allegations against suspects when they are arrested and broadcast press conferences in which prosecutors and police do their best to demonstrate the defendant's guilt.

As a practical matter, even if a defendant is acquitted at trial, he still doesn't receive the benefit of the presumption of innocence, because if he did, the state would owe him compensation for accusing and trying him for a crime he didn't commit. But, of course, a not-guilty verdict doesn't mean that the defendant is innocent: it just means that the jury had a reasonable doubt about his guilt.

In short, it is ridiculous to claim that a person accused of a crime is considered innocent until proven guilty at any time, except at start of the trial. The next time you hear somebody repeat this nonsense, I hope you will be able to straighten him out.

Another shop-worn phrase associated with criminal law is "guilt beyond a reasonable doubt." What exactly does this mean? The concept is very hard to define, even for lawyers. Actually, the *judges* don't have a much better grasp of this slippery notion. Here are a few examples:

From the Ninth Circuit of the U.S. Court of Appeals *Manual of Model Jury Instructions*:

"Proof beyond a reasonable doubt is proof that leaves you firmly convinced the defendant is guilty. It is not required that the government prove guilt beyond all possible doubt... A reasonable doubt is a doubt based upon reason and common sense and is not based purely on speculation. It may arise from a careful and impartial consideration of all the evidence, or from lack of evidence."

Well, that certainly clears it up for me.

Here's what the Cornell Law School Legal Information Institute has to say about on the subject:

"The prosecution must convince the jury that there is no other reasonable explanation that can come from the evidence presented at trial. In other words, the jury must be virtually certain of the defendant's guilt in order to render a guilty verdict."

"Virtually certain," hmm. Sounds like a pretty high bar. I guarantee that no defense attorney in Pennsylvania would *ever* be permitted to offer this definition to a jury, because that's not what the *Pennsylvania Standard Jury Instructions* say. According to the latter:

"A reasonable doubt is a doubt that would cause a reasonably careful and sensible person to hesitate before acting upon a matter of importance in his own affairs."

That's really helpful, isn't it?

The concept is so amorphous that some federal courts simply refuse to define reasonable doubt in their jury instructions, leaving it to twelve persons untrained in the law to figure out what it means for themselves:

"Reasonable doubt is a fundamental concept that does not easily lend itself to refinement or definition." United States v. Vavlitis, 9 F.3d 206. No kidding.

"[A]n instruction which uses the words "reasonable doubt" without further definition adequately apprises the jury of the proper burden of proof." United States v. Olmstead, 832 F.2d 642.

Oh, does it, does it? If it's as simple as that, why not explain it to the jury?

"[T]he greatest wisdom may lie with the Fourth Circuit's and Seventh Circuit's instruction to leave to juries the task of deliberating the meaning of reasonable doubt." United States v. Taylor, 997 F.2d 1551. Or, if not "the greatest wisdom," possibly the greatest abdication of responsibility.

In short, the meaning of reasonable doubt is so indefinite that the judges charged with explaining the law to ordinary people, judges of the Federal Circuit Courts, mind you, admit that *they* can't define it, so they wash their hands of all responsibility for helping juries to understand this "fundamental concept." Considering that reasonable doubt is not something that most people use in everyday life, this is a serious dereliction of duty on the part of judges who are just one step below the Supreme Court.

Commentary: The Child Sex Abuse Panic

Despite concepts like "innocent until proven guilty," "proof beyond a reasonable doubt," and "the burden of proof is always on the prosecution," criminal cases are almost always an uphill fight for the defense. Common sense tells you that the defendant wouldn't have been arrested if there wasn't a good reason to think he had done something, and that he wouldn't be on trial, if there wasn't some pretty good evidence against him.

This problem is more acute in some kinds of cases than in others. It is a particular issue in charges of child sex abuse (CSA). This has always been true to some extent, but ever since the 1980s and '90s and the massive publicity generated by the "satanic ritual abuse" and pre-school day care hysteria, anyone accused of this crime was guilty until proven innocent. Although the existence of satanic ritual abuse (SRA) was eventually debunked, this was only after more than 12,000 people been charged with participation in sexual abuse cults in the U.S., and not a single one substantiated by police. Moreover, in all but a tiny handful of these cases, the charges were either dropped before they came to trial, ended in acquittals or, if the trial resulted in a conviction, were subsequently overturned on appeal. Nonetheless, the massive coverage of these SRA cases in the media produced a moral panic in the area of child sex abuse with an effect on public perceptions that is still with us today. The CSA hysteria subsequently became a world-wide phenomenon, spreading to Western Europe, the UK, and other English-peaking countries, such as Australia and New Zealand. Recently, there has also been a revival of politically inspired ritual abuse conspiracies by the QAnon cult.

It all started with the McMartin Pre-School Abuse case, which produced the longest and most expensive criminal trial in U.S. history (seven years and $15,000,000, respectively) and resulted in no convictions, but did ruin the lives of the defendants and traumatized hundreds of children. The case also begat a string of accusations against employees and operators of pre-school day care centers all over the country.

By employing suggestive, leading questions and coercive interviewing tactics on very young children, and refusing to believe the children when they denied that any abuse had taken place, prosecution "expert," Kee McFarland, obtained often bizarre descriptions of cult-like sexual activities from the alleged victims. In 1984, a grand jury indicted seven defendants, all of who worked at the McMartin Pre-school at one time or another: Ray Buckey, Peggy Buckey (Ray's mother), Peggy Ann Buckey (Ray's sister), Virginia McMartin, and three teachers, Mary Ann Jackson, Bette Raidor, and Babette Spitler, and charged them numerous counts of sex abuse.

After a preliminary hearing that lasted more than a year (!), the charges against all of the defendants except Ray and Peggy Buckey were dropped by the District Attorney. Before the trial began, a member of the prosecution team revealed that the original complainant had been unable to identify the chief defendant, Ray Buckey in a lineup, and that his mother, Judy Johnson, was suffering from paranoid schizophrenia at the time she brought the charges to the police.

At the trial of the two remaining defendants, children testified that they had been sexually assaulted by the defendants on farms, in circuses, in car washes, churches, grocery stores and in a secret room in the day care building (the building consisted of one room, with windows on all sides, and no closets). It was also claimed that abuse took place in underground tunnels at the day care site, that the defendants had used the children to make pornographic films, and had sacrificed animals and forced the victims to drink their blood. One witness claimed he had been sexually abused on the altar of a church. Another claimed that he had seen Ray Buckey kill a horse with a baseball bat at the school, and one boy identified actor Chuck Norris as being one of his abusers. One accusation against Ray Buckey was by a boy who had not attended the school during the time Buckey had worked there. No physical evidence of any kind, tunnels, animals, pornography, or anything else, was ever found, nor was any medical evidence of the abuse ever produced.

The defense showed videotapes of Kee McFarland's interviews, where she consistently refused to believe the children when they denied being abused, and repeatedly asked leading questions until they gave her the desired answers. Both defendants took the stand and denied every charge.

In the end, the jury found Peggy Buckey not guilty on all charges, and Ray Buckey not guilty on all but 13 counts, on which they were deadlocked. He was retried on eight of the thirteen counts, and once again, the jury was unable to reach a unanimous verdict. Finally, the prosecutor decided against a third trial, and the remaining charges against Ray Buckey were dropped. All it had cost the defendants was their life savings, homes, careers and reputations. Ray Buckey spent five years in prison, most of it in pre-trial detention.

The McMartin case proved to be only the first of many child sex abuse cases brought against the employees of day care centers all over the country in the next few years. The fact that none of the defendants had been found guilty of any crime did nothing to discourage the media from promoting the SRA hysteria. For example, after the first McMartin trial, Geraldo Rivera hosted several children and their parents on a show devoted to "The McMartin Outrage," featuring children who insisted that they had been molested at the school by the defendants. One of them, Chris Collins, "remembered" being assaulted by Ray Buckey and witnessing satanic ritual animal sacrifices conducted by Buckey in an underground room below the school in the mid-1970s. However, Buckey was still in high school at the time, and his school records showed that he had perfect attendance, meaning that he could not possibly have been present at the pre-school during the time Collins was there. (See: *The McMartin Preschool Abuse Trial: An Account* by Professor Douglas O. Linder https://famous-trials.com/mcmartin/902-home.)

At around the same time as the McMartin trial was the Kern County, California case, in which 36 people were convicted of child sex abuse as part of a Satanic sex ring. Most of the defendants spent time in prison before the all convictions but two were overturned by appellate courts (the two exceptions were defendants who died in prison before their appeals could be heard.)

Among many other such prosecutions was the 1992 Oak Hill case, where a husband and wife were convicted of multiple counts of child sex abuse by the same methods used in the McMartin case. They were sentenced to 48 years in prison. Further investigation by the county DA's office revealed that the convictions had been obtained with false testimony by a medical expert, the withholding of exculpatory evidence from the defense, and "recovered memory" testimony. The defendants were declared to be "actually innocent" by the DA's office, and released, after spending 21 years in state prison. (See: *The Ritual Sex Abuse Hoax* by Debbie Nathan , the Village Voice, Jan. 12, 1990, http://ncrj.org/resources/info/the-ritual-sex-abuse-hoax/)

The creation of the "recovered memory" movement was one more consequence of the RSA panic. Recovered Memory Therapy (RMT) was a psychological technique that claimed to restore memories that had been buried in the minds of victims of childhood sexual assault. RTM therapists claim that lost or suppressed memories can be restored by use of hypnosis, drugs (such as sodium amytal,) past life regression and other methods, claims have been debunked to the extent that recovered memory testimony is not considered reliable enough to be used as evidence in Federal courts or most state courts. These recovered memories rarely if ever can be collaborated by objective evidence, and when such evidence is available, it almost always contradicts the supposed memory. It is now widely accepted among psychologists, other than proponents of RMT, that memory does not function in the way described by RMT theory. Experience teaches us that, rather than forget or repress traumatic events, they are more difficult to forget than most other things. For example, soldiers' memories of combat are burned into their minds to the extent that veterans suffer from Post Traumatic Stress Disorder, because they are *unable* to forget the horrible memories of combat.

It has since been shown that these so-called recovered memories are the result of suggestions by therapists, who already believe their patients problems are the result of traumatic childhood sex abuse. RMT evidence was the basis for many CSA prosecutions, some (but not all) of which were subsequently overturned. What's more, despite the weight of scientific evidence against it, RMT is sometimes still today by some courts, if the case has received sufficient publicity. (See: *The false memory syndrome: Experimental studies and comparison to confabulations*, M.F. Mendez and I.A. Fras, https://www.ncbi.nlm.nih.gov/pmc/articles/PMC3143501)

Recovered memory therapy and recovered memories played a major role part of the prosecution evidence against the retired Penn State football coach Jerry Sandusky. A subsequent investigation revealed that, in addition to RMT evidence, the case against Sandusky was riddled with glaring factual inconsistencies and fabrications, during a trial that took place in an atmosphere of overwhelmingly toxic publicity. (See: Mark Prendergast, *The Most Hated Man in America: Jerry Sandusky and the Rush to Judgment*.) I confess that before I read Prendergast's book, I like 99.9% of America, believed Sandusky was guilty. After reading Prendergast's account, I have no doubt that he was another victim of the moral panic that started 40 years ago with the McMartin day care case.

Eleven: Not a Standard Case

According to the American Bar Association, "a lawyer must ...act with commitment and dedication to the interests of the client and with zeal in advocacy upon the client's behalf." (Rule 3.1 ABA *Model Rules of Professional Conduct*). In the course of my career, I tried to live up to this standard, but I will admit that I was not always successful. There were some clients who I disliked so much that I could not provide the proper "zeal in advocacy" expected of me. This may seem surprising, given the fact that I generally had no problem representing all sorts of violent criminal lowlifes, including accused child molesters. Usually this was caused by personal experiences that made me overly-sensitive to certain type of crimes and/or individuals.

I will give one example from juvenile court. I was appointed to represent a thirteen-year-old girl who was charged with simple assault, which didn't sound like anything too serious. The facts, as confirmed by the client, were as follows. She was in a hallway at her school, engaged in changing classes, when she passed another girl, a classmate who was asking for trouble, because she was a "show off" who answered questions in class, got 'A's on the tests, was on the honor roll, and regularly committed other, similar provocations against my client. For these reasons, my client proceeded to knock the schoolbooks out of her classmate's arms and scatter her papers all over the hallway, then administered a good thumping to the offender. The client finished up by picking her classmate up, and stuffing her face-first into a tall waste can. My client was completely unrepentant, stating her opinion that the other girl deserved what she got.

I have had a very strong dislike of bullies ever since I was the victim of them in elementary and junior high school, and I do not know what I would have done if I had been obliged to defend this girl at an adjudicatory hearing, because I could not think about her case rationally: I hated her. Fortunately for all concerned, my commitment and dedication to the client was not put to too stern a test. She admitted to the crime, and as this was not her first such offense, she was found to be in need of treatment, supervision or rehabilitation. I forget exactly what the court did with her, but I believe she was shipped off to a medium-secure juvenile facility, which probably did not improve her behavior in any significant way.

The other case that comes to mind when I think of occasions when I may not have provided the client with the most zealous possible representation, is Commonwealth v. Devin White. On one hand, I took advantage of some dumb luck to get him acquitted of the most serious charges, but on the other ...well, after you read the story of this case, you can decide for yourself whether I acted properly as White's attorney.

Devin White was driving around West Philadelphia, minding his own business, when he ran a red light at 56th and Spruce. This was very careless of him, as this was only 2 short blocks away from the 18th Police District, and he was observed by police who were sitting in their cruiser drinking coffee when White ignored the traffic signal. It was particularly imprudent behavior, because, when the police ran the license plate, they discovered that the car had been reported stolen three days earlier.

Matters then took their usual course, and approximately six months later, I, in company with Assistant District Attorney Jan McAfee, found myself in the robing room of Judge Nelson Cruz, to hear Ms. McAfee's motion to add an information charging Mr. White with Criminal Conspiracy to the existing charges, these being Robbery Causing Physical Injury a Felony of the 2nd Degree, Theft by Taking (Motor Vehicle) and Receiving Stolen Property (Motor Vehicle), both Felonies of the 3rd Degree, and Simple Assault, a Misdemeanor of the 2nd Degree. This was the second day of the trial. We had spent the whole first day picking a jury, and were scheduled to deliver opening statements, when Ms. McAfee brought this new charge to the attention of the court.

Somebody, whether it was Jan or someone else in her office had really screwed the pooch on this on, because her motion to amend the charges was too late. "Your Honor," I said, "under the rules, the prosecution can't add any charges now, after we have picked the jury." This was true, under the Rules of Criminal Procedure at that time. (The rules have since been amended to allow the prosecutor to add new charges at any time before both sides have rested.)

Judge Cruz turned to Ms. McAfee. "I think Mr. Heller is correct, Ms. McAfee. The issue has been joined, and no new counts may be added at this stage." This mistake gave me an opening to save something from what had looked like a dead loser of a case.

The facts of the case were not complicated. The complaining witness was a Mr. Lee, a recent immigrant from Korea, who had been brought over to the States by his brother-in-law to work at the latter's store. As a stranger in a strange land, he was quite naturally lonely, particularly for female companionship. Despite his less than perfect command of English, he was able to communicate his desire for a "date" and his ability to pay for the experience to Devin White. White promised to introduce Mr. Lee to an accommodating young lady who would perform the desired services for a reasonable fee.

They got into Mr. Lee's car and drove together to Tasker Homes, a housing project in South Philadelphia. Once there White took his new friend down into a basement, directed him to a door, and politely invited Mr. Lee to precede him. As soon as Lee entered the room, someone pulled a bag over his head, and he was soundly beaten by one or more unseen assailants until he was lying on the floor in a state of semi-consciousness. Whereupon persons unknown went through his pockets and took his wallet and car keys, then left him there. Fortunately, he was not seriously injured, and only suffered cuts, bruises and minor lacerations.

I had just a couple of questions on cross-examination (which he answered, as he had on direct, through an interpreter.)

Me: There were three other people in the room with you, correct?

Witness: Yes.

Me: And you know that because you heard three people talking, right?

Witness: Yes.

Me: Mr. Lee, could you see which of them hit you?

Witness: No.

Me: Could you see who went through your pockets?

Witness: No, I couldn't see anything.

Me: You don't know how many people hit you, do you?

Witness: No.

Me: It might have been one?

Witness: I think it was two that hit me.

Me: And you can't say if Mr. White was one of those two, can you?

Witness: No. I couldn't see who did it.

Me: And you don't know if Mr. White was the one who went through your pockets, either, do you?

Witness: It might have been two that went through my pockets.

Me: But you cannot say if Mr. White was one of them, can you?

Witness: No.

Me: No more questions.

I had what I needed, thanks to the missing conspiracy charge.

As soon as the Commonwealth rested, I moved for a judgement of acquittal under 606 (A) (1) of the Pennsylvania Rules of Criminal Procedure, asking the judge to find that the Commonwealth had failed to produce sufficient evidence to sustain a conviction on three of the four counts. This motion is almost automatic for the defense, even where the evidence is actually sufficient, or even overwhelming, and is normally denied just as automatically. In this case, however, I thought I stood a decent chance of having the motion granted (which would have been a first for me.)

It wasn't granted, though. "I understand your arguments, Mr. Heller," Judge Cruz said, "but I am not inclined to take the case away from the jury…at this point."

I was not too disappointed. I took the judge's last three words as an indication that he would consider granting a motion for a directed verdict in favor of Mr. White, if the jury somehow reached the wrong result (that is, a verdict of guilty).

So, it was left up to me to explain the matter to the jury in my closing statement, which I did as follows:

"Let's examine each of the four charges against Mr. White against the standard of guilt beyond a reasonable doubt, and see if we can't clear up this case. First of all, I would ask you to consider Count Four, Receiving Stolen Property (Motor Vehicle) a Felony of the 3rd Degree. This charge is based on the undisputed facts that Devin White was arrested while in possession of Mr. Lee's car, and that he lacked any permission or authority to do so. Devin

White is unquestionably guilty of this crime, and you should so find, when you go back to deliberate.

"But what about the other three counts, of Robbery, Theft by Taking and Simple Assault? Did the Commonwealth prove *those* beyond a reasonable doubt? The answer is no. There is no question that my client took Mr. Lee to that room in the basement of a building in the Tasker Homes project, and based on the evidence your heard in this trial, you may reasonably conclude that he knew two other people were waiting for him to bring Mr. Lee there, so that they could rob him. If Mr. White had been charged with Criminal Conspiracy in connection with this case, the circumstantial evidence that he conspired to commit Robbery, Theft by Taking, and Simple Assault with those two unknown persons would be sufficient to prove him guilty of those crimes, beyond a reasonable doubt.

"But, for reasons best known to the Commonwealth, there is no charge of conspiracy before you..." [because somebody in the DA's office had fornicated the canine, but I wasn't about to tell the jury that] ... "which means that in order to find Devin White guilty of Robbery, Theft by Taking, or Simple Assault, you would need proof that he personally committed the acts that constitute these offenses, and you do not have it.

"Mr. Lee testified that he believed there were three people in the room with him, and two of them hit and kicked him, but he could not see who they were. Fortunately, he was not seriously injured. This is Simple Assault, a Misdemeanor of the 2nd

Degree. Mr. Lee also told you that two people went through his pockets to relieve him of his wallet and car keys, which constitutes Theft by Taking, but once again, when I asked him if he could identify those persons, he honestly answered that he was unable to see who they were. More specifically, he could not tell us whether Devin White had done either thing. Theft by Taking plus Simple Assault makes a Robbery, a Felony of the 2nd Degree.

"Now, in order to reach a verdict of guilty on these charges, you must first find that Devin White *personally* assaulted Mr. Lee, and that he was one of the two people who went through Mr. Lee's pockets. If this was a racetrack or a casino, rather than a criminal trial, the odds that Mr. White was one of the two assailants would be excellent: 2 to 1, in fact. If his guilt depended on you finding that it was more likely than not that he committed these crimes, then your task would be simple. If you only needed to find that he *probably* was guilty, then two to one odds would be more than sufficient.

"But *probably* is not good enough here. In a criminal case, in order to reach a verdict of guilty, you must conclude that he committed the offenses charged *beyond a reasonable doubt*. Not 'maybe,' not 'perhaps,' not 'probably,' but beyond a reasonable doubt. And a 1 out of 3 chance that he did not personally and individually assault or rob Mr. Lee is the very definition of reasonable doubt. The evidence in this case can get you no further than suspicion; it cannot and does not reach to the high standard of beyond a reasonable doubt. So, for the reasons I have stated, I ask you to do your collective duty, and find Devin White guilty of Receiving Stolen Property, and not guilty of Robbery, Theft by Taking, and Simple Assault."

Jan McAfee gave it the old college try, attempting to persuade the jury that they should not let the defense attorney steal away their prerogative by telling them what to do.

"Just because Mr. Heller says something doesn't make it a fact. It is not up to him to decide what the defendant is or is not guilty of; it is entirely up to you. It's obvious that Devin White planned this entire crime with his two..."

Me: Objection. There is not a scintilla of evidence about who planned anything.

Court: Objection sustained. The jury will disregard the statement by Ms. McAfee. You may continue.

McAfee: Regardless of that, it is as plain as can be that Devin White was an absolutely essential actor in every single thing that happened to...

Me: Objection. There was no evidence that my client was essential in every single thing that happened.

Court: Sustained. The jury will disregard. Please move on, Ms. McAfee...

Suffice it to say that the course of Ms. McAfee's closing argument did not run smoothly. Nor were either of us surprised when the jury returned with a verdict of not guilty on Robbery, Theft by Taking, and Simple Assault, and guilty on Theft: Receiving Stolen Property.

One month later, I was back in court for Devin White's sentencing hearing. While we waited for

Judge Cruz to appear, Jan McAfee, who was sitting next to me, remarked, "Your client is a real piece of crap, Mr. Heller," an observation with which I did not venture to disagree. "He's not even going to get state time for this robbery. The standard guideline sentence for RSP..." [Receiving Stolen Property] ... "is only 6 ½ to 11 months."

A word of explanation is probably useful here. The Commonwealth of Pennsylvania publishes guidelines for judges to follow when sentencing defendants, in an effort to ensure that the sentences are, if not fair, at least similar for defendants convicted of the same crimes in the various jurisdictions, so that a defendant convicted of RSP in Center County, let's say, will not catch 2 ½ to 5 years upstate, while one in Philadelphia with a similar criminal history is sent away for only 6 to 11 ½ months in county custody. Since Devin White had no prior adult history, and his fairly extensive juvenile history could not be used against him (well, he hadn't had time to run up much of an adult record, since he was only 19 when he was arrested for this case,) he normally would be sentenced under the "standard" range for first offenders on an RSP conviction.

I thought about that, then said something I wasn't supposed to. "Well, Jan," I said, "this isn't exactly a standard case, is it?"

She stared at me. "What do you mean, exactly?"

"I mean," I went on, further burying my client, "just because he wasn't charged with conspiracy to commit robbery, theft, and simple assault doesn't mean that the judge can't consider the circumstances of the case when he imposes sentences. Now, if I were the prosecutor in this case, I think I would bring that to the court's attention."

She nodded. "I think you would, Mr. Heller," she said.

Imagine my dismay when the case was called for the sentencing hearing, and Jan McAfee started out with, "Your Honor, I realize that the standard guideline range in this case is 6 1/2 to 11, but this is not a standard case…" I was even more shocked when Devin White was sentenced to 1 ½ to 3 years in a state correctional facility. Oh, well. Over the years, I have learned to be philosophical about such disappointments. You win some and you lose some…and sometimes you do both at the same time.

Snapshot: A Gentleman and a Plumber

I would be remiss if I did not tell you about a now-deceased friend, who was surely one of the most unusual lawyers ever to appear in the annals of the Philadelphia court system, Victor M. Snyder [real name], generally known to friends and foes alike (he had lots of the latter,) as "Vic."

I met Vic a few years before his death in 2001, so much of what I think I know about his life before I met him comes from him, and as Vic enjoyed pulling your leg, until it came off in his hand, I can't guarantee the accuracy of everything he told me about himself. He grew up in a tough, working-class Philadelphia neighborhood, and was either orphaned or lost his father at a young age. This deduction is based on the fact that he was a graduate of Girard College, a Philadelphia boarding school established by Stephen Girard in 1833, to quote Girard's will, "for poor, white, orphan, males." (Orphan was interpreted by the courts as meaning "fatherless.") At Girard College, the students were required not only to complete the rigorous academic program, but also learn a trade. Vic's trade was plumbing, and after he graduated in 1958, he served an apprenticeship to a master plumber. At some point after he graduated from high school, he volunteered to serve in the Army, and saw combat in 1965 in Vietnam at the notorious Battle of Ia Drang Valley.

After he obtained his master plumber license, he started his own company. Vic Snyder Plumbing quickly became the largest residential plumbing company in Philadelphia. Much of this was due to the company's television and radio advertising campaign, for which Vic wrote most of the copy himself. I can remember one of his commercials that promised "You'll flush with pride with Vic Snyder plumbing." Another ad started this way: "Ever since Sir Thomas Crapper invented the flush toilet in 1880..."

Among his other exploits, he was part of a Mt. Everest expedition (it failed to reach the summit due to bad weather). He also did some skydiving in his spare time. At some point, he decided to go back to school to earn a college degree, which he did, earning a BA in history from Temple University in 1976, while still running his plumbing business. According to Vic, his business was in court so frequently, both as a defendant and a plaintiff in suits with his customers, that he decided it would more economical if he became a lawyer himself to save on legal fees.

He graduated from Temple Law School in 1980, with considerable assistance (again, according to Vic himself) from the president of Temple, Peter Liacouras, who was a friend from the old neighborhood. Vic was far from stupid, but his brand of native intelligence did not translate well to the academic sphere, as was shown by the fact that he failed the bar examination on his first five tries.

Not all of Vic Snyder's legal troubles were in the civil courts. He was arrested and charged with felony theft by deception and conspiracy in 1983, before he had managed to pass the bar examination, and these charges, which were eventually dismissed, prevented him from taking the test 1983. These difficulties were described in the February 18, 1983, *Philadelphia Daily News* under a headline reading "Drain on His Patience: Vic Snyder Barred from the Bar Exam."

He ran afoul of the law again in 1994 (from the *Philadelphia Daily News*, December 17, 1993):

"Philadelphia plumber-turned-lawyer Vic Snyder has been accused of clogging justice. Cops say he asked two official court translators to lie if his client gave the wrong story in court. Snyder plunged into hot water Wednesday, surrendering to District Attorney's Detective Joseph A. Murphy on two counts of soliciting perjury and soliciting false swearing. Since prosecutors are throwing everything but the kitchen sink at Snyder, the crimes could cost him his law license if he's convicted." (As you can see, the reporters didn't miss many opportunities to work in plumbing references.)

These charges were dismissed by a Municipal Court judge at the preliminary hearing with these words: "The inference I draw is that Mr. Snyder doesn't know how to try a criminal case. It cries out for mandatory (legal) education. But it doesn't tell me his intent was to lie." (*Philadelphia Daily News*, February 23, 1994.)

Say what you will about him, when Vic Snyder entered a room, people noticed. He was of average height and build. His hair was white and clipped short. He had bad skin and a nose that had clearly been broken more than once. But what cannot be caught in words was the *impression* he made. You could not ignore him. Although he knew as little law as any attorney I have ever known, he dominated courtrooms with his bigger than life personality. Juries saw him as the common man personified, and when he antagonized prosecutors and judges, jurors would side with Vic and his clients. He had an enviable record of success in spite of a reputation as a legal ignoramus. He was constantly in trouble with judges for his impulsive words and actions. I don't know exactly how many times he was held in contempt, but it was more than once...a lot more.

If you think of a trial as a battle of wits, an intellectual duel, when Vic Snyder was involved, it was more like an all-in wrestling match, complete with bodies being hurled through the ropes and folding chairs being thrown wildly around. All sorts of stories were told about him around the Criminal Justice Factory, and the chances are good that Vic started them. Here's my favorite:

It was the afternoon, in the middle of a narcotics case. The court had taken a short recess (for the witnesses and lawyers to take a leak, catch a smoke, etc.) but when the presiding judge returned to the bench, there was no sign of Vic's client.

"Mr. Snyder," the judge asked, "I see that your client has not returned. Do you know where he is?"

He looked around, did not see the client anywhere in the courtroom, thought for a moment, then exclaimed, "Your Honor, I think the police murdered him!"

Snapshot: Kissing Ass for Fun and Profit

One technique for winning trials that they don't teach in law school is sucking up to the judge. This method works much better for the prosecution, for reasons I have already made plain in great detail and, probably, tiresome length.

In any case, I am basically a bomb-throwing anarchist at heart, and I react badly to authority figures, like judges, as these memoirs have amply demonstrated. (Of course, judges don't seem to be crazy about me, either.)

The opposite side of judicial ass-kissing, is judge-baiting, one of Vic Snyder's favorite pastimes. I once warned him that this was a dangerous sport. "Better than no sport at all," he told me. Below are a few examples of both.

When I was with the Kings County DA, we followed a practice called "open file discovery (OFD)." This meant that we prosecutors were supposed to hand over copies of everything in our case files to the defense. But there were limits even to open file discovery. One of these had to do with releasing certain personal information about our victims to the other side, which might be used by a defendant to harass or intimidate the complaining witness.

Normally, I didn't worry too much about such things. To me, it seemed unlikely that anybody would get that worked up over the cases they gave us first-year ADAs. But there was this one time...

I had inherited the case from a colleague, and he had decided to withhold some report, interview, *something* from the OFD, and the Legal Aid attorney on the other side wanted that something. We appeared before the assigned judge to thrash out the matter. This judge was an ancient legal ignoramus, and had the disposition of a junkyard dog with a bad toothache. I hated him on first sight.

"All right, Mr. Heller," the judge growled at me, "I am ordering you to hand over the discovery requested by the defense."

The truth was, I could not have cared less about the discovery item, whatever it was. I just disliked being pushed around. "I'm sorry Your Honor," I lied, "but I can't. It's not discovery under the Rules of Criminal Procedure (the 'RCP')."

This was both true and misleading. The RCP listed items of *mandatory* discovery that we had to turn over (such as investigation reports, property receipts, and so forth.) But the RCP only laid down the minimum requirements. It did not forbid us from giving the defense more that.

As I had suspected, the learned judge wasn't up on his Criminal Procedure. This hardly mattered, as he didn't have much use for the little law he knew. Anyway, he had something better: "I don't care *what* the Rules say," he bellowed, his face darkening visibly (which is more impressive when you realize that the judge was African-American.) He stood halfway up behind the bench, then leaned forward to add, "I *order* you to turn over the discovery immediately, right *now*!"

It occurred to me that if he was pushed a little further, he might have an aneurysm and drop dead on the spot. I visualized the old monster flopping forward over the bench in his death throes. It made an attractive picture.

I had fully intended to turn over the item in any case, but this seemed like too good an opportunity to improve the quality of the Criminal Court judges to let pass. So, I said, "I wish I could, Your Honor, but I can't. Anyway, this is not a particularly important case, is it? It's only a marijuana charge."

"Unimportant?" he demanded, more outraged than ever. "Marijuana is the most serious crime we have!"

I realized that I had met my match, and it was time to run up the white flag. Anybody who believed that marijuana constituted a greater danger to society than arson, murder, or rape, was seriously deranged, and I no desire to cross swords with a lunatic.

"Your Honor, I am handing over the discovery now," I said, matching the deed to the word. Then I excused myself and got out of there.

For an outstanding performance of blatant osculation of a judicial posterior in my experience, I offer you this exchange from a charging conference with Judge Cheever (remember him from Time Cops?) We had just finished up the evidence, and were now discussing what jury instructions (other than the standard ones) each side wanted. [If you're wondering what the case was about, I can't help you. I have completely forgotten it.]

In the course of this discussion, out of the blue, and apropos of absolutely nothing, the ADA puckered up and said, "Judge Cheever, I just want to say what a wonderful job you are doing handling this trial."

He stared at her, perhaps wondering if she was actually serious.

I was not about to let the prosecution get away with anything. "That's a very handsome tie you're wearing today, Your Honor," I told him.

Some are born ass-kissers, some are made ass-kissers, and some have ass-kissing thrust upon them. I had occasion to fall into the third category.

It was like this: I was doing a robbery case before Judge James Linebarger [real name] a judge with whom I had not gotten along well in the past, which hardly made him unique in my experience. But somehow, during a long delay in the proceedings, we got to talking about World War II, and we discovered that we were both military history geeks. I have a Master's degree in European History, and the judge was a Vietnam veteran who received a battlefield commission, and left the service with the rank of captain, after starting out as an enlisted man.

He was tickled pink when he found that I could converse knowledgably about such important legal issues as the Eastern Front, the North Africa campaign, and the generalship of Vinegar Joe Stilwell. It got to the point where the judge almost forgot that the prosecutor (a decent sort, if memory serves) even existed. When the poor fellow tried to join in the military history chat the judge and I were having (something for which he was pathetically unprepared: he didn't know a Heinkel He-111 medium bomber from a hole in the ground, a Panzer IV from a postman, or an LST from LSD,) we pretty much ignored him. I can't say I didn't enjoy the sensation of being buddies with the judge for a change.

In the end, mainly due to the failure of several Commonwealth witnesses to appear, the jury found my client not guilty on six of the eight robbery counts against him. Judge Linebarger beamed down at me, and said, "This is a tremendous victory for you, Mr. Heller." This was the one and only time in my career when a judge congratulated me on a result.

Did my temporary friendship with the judge have any effect on the outcome of the case? Probably not, but it was nice not to have to swim against the current for once.

I will end by telling you about my first trial in Philadelphia. More specifically, I want to introduce you to a judge who made the Brooklyn Criminal Court lunatic at the beginning of this section look like a saint by comparison.

The charge was aggravated assault. The ADA was (you guessed it!) Jan McAfee. The judge was Angelo Guarino [real name].

Guarino had been on the bench since shortly after the Civil War. When he reached the mandatory retirement age, he was permitted to keep hearing cases as a Senior Judge. But his mistreatment of everyone in his courtroom, including his own staff, was so vile that he had been temporarily removed from the bench -- twice. This was after he had punished potential jurors for their answers to his questions during the jury selection process.

He had only recently been permitted to hear cases again when my case came before him. It did not take long for Judge Guarino to demonstrate his contempt for the Supreme Court that had *dared* to remove him

This would be a good place to describe the jury selection process for those of you who have never gone through it yourselves. The method used in Pennsylvania is much as in the rest of the United States, with minor local variations.

To begin with, the names are culled from various lists within the county (or in the case of federal courts, the federal district,) such as registered voters and licensed drivers. The chosen ones are sent letters informing them on the date on which they must appear at the county courthouse (in Philadelphia, the Criminal Justice Center.) Once there, the potential jurors answer questions on 2-page forms they are given. The first part of the form asks for personal information, about their employment, level of education, age, etc. The second page poses a series of questions specific to jury duty, such as whether they are willing to follow the judge's instructions on the law, to deliberate with others and still make up your own mind, believe police officers are more (or less) credible than civilians, and so forth. Finally, they are asked if there is some personal reason that they cannot serve.

When a panel of venirepersons (from the English common law "*venire fascias*", a writ ordering a person for service on a jury,) is called up to a courtroom, copies of these forms are distributed to the judge, defense attorney and prosecutor. The next step is called *voir dire*, questioning of the panelists for their fitness to serve on a jury. What happens now depends almost entirely on the judge. Some judges simply turn the whole process over to the lawyers, and only intervene when one of them raises an objection. Others limit the *voir dire* in some way, whether by number of questions, subjects of the questions, or in some other way. Some judges, like Guarino, take the *voir dire* almost entirely away from the lawyers, and conduct all the questioning themselves. The only role played by the attorneys is to tell the judge whether the juror is acceptable, or if they wish to challenge him/her.

Back to my case. One of the venirepersons had checked the box on the form indicating that she believed police officers were less truthful than civilian witnesses. Guarino told the woman that a juror should not assume that any witness, police or civilian, is automatically more or less credible because of his job, then asked her if she understood that. The panelist agreed that she did.

Then he asked if she now wanted to change the answer she made on the form, that she particularly distrusted police officers. He clearly expected the woman to say "yes." Instead, she answered, "In my experience, police officers can't be trusted to tell the truth."

"If I tell you that you must apply the same standards to evaluate every witness, no matter what his job is, will you be able to do that?" He asked, already sounding irritated. Guarino didn't care what she *really* believed, he just wanted to make sure she could not escape jury duty by giving the lawyers a reason to dismiss her because she might not be fair.

The woman thought his question over it for a few seconds, then said, "No, Your Honor, I'm not sure I could change what I believe so easily."

When the woman dared to contradict him to his face, Guarino exploded. "Madam, I am *ordering* you follow my instructions that you must not give any extra weight to the testimony of any witness because of his job!" he yelled. "Do you understand that, or do I need to make myself clearer?" He demanded menacingly.

I was not surprised to hear the unfortunate woman faintly agree that she understood, nor to see her sink shakily back down in her seat.

Having now, he thought, disposed of any possible objection to the panelist's fitness to serve, Guarino turned to me. "Is this juror acceptable to the defense?" He asked.

Anybody who distrusted the police as much as this woman probably been a very good juror for the defense, but I was so pissed off by the way the old dragon had browbeaten her into submission, that I said, "I move she be excused for cause. She clearly stated that she could not be fair in evaluating the testimony of police officers."

"Both counsel to sidebar," he said. When we got there, he glared me and snarled, "What is your challenge for cause, Mr. Heller?"

"Your Honor, the woman made it crystal clear that she could not be fair to both sides..."

"But then I rehabilitated her," Guarino interrupted, "and she changed her mind."

"With all due respect, Your Honor," I said, only barely holding onto my temper, "you didn't *rehabilitate* her; you just intimidated her, so she would say whatever you wanted!"

Now it was Guarino's turn to be outraged, or to at least to simulate that emotion. "What do you mean?" he shouted. "I never intimidated a witness in my life!" [He was so excited by my accusation that he actually said "witness," instead of "juror."]

He turned to Jan McAfee, who had been profoundly silent during my exchange with the judge. "Ms. McAfee, did *I* intimidate that woman?" He asked.

Jan looked at me, glanced in the direction of the jury box, then back at Guarino. She said, "No, Your Honor, you didn't intimidate her."

I didn't blame her then for that answer, nor did I hold it against her later. There are just certain times when you don't have a choice about kissing a judicial bottom, and this was one of them.

This, my first trial in Philadelphia, also had the distinction of being the last one for Guarino, at least it was the last one he finished. His abusive behavior became so bad that he was removed from the bench *in the middle* of his next trial and replaced with another judge, something I have never heard of before or since. Here is that story, as summarized in the opinion of the U.S. Third Circuit Court in Guarino v. Larsen, et al, 11 F.3d 1151 (1993):

"After serving for seventeen years on the Philadelphia Court of Common Pleas, Judge Guarino retired upon his 70th birthday [The mandatory retirement age] ... He then applied for designation as a senior judge [and was] certified that he met the requirements for senior status under Rule 701 of the Pennsylvania Rules of Judicial Administration...The court assigned Judge Guarino for a one-month term beginning on March 24, 1991, and renewed that assignment for each month through November of 1992. The only exception was a ten-day period in April of 1992. It is undisputed that the court delayed renewal of Judge Guarino's assignment for that ten-day period in April 1992 as a result of its concerns about a class action suit that had been filed on March 19, 1982, against Judge Guarino in the United States District Court for the Eastern District of Pennsylvania...

"The named plaintiffs [in the class-action suit] included two persons who Judge Guarino thought had attempted to avoid jury duty by giving false answers during *voir dire*. As punishment, Judge Guarino had required these venirepersons to return to the courtroom for an additional day as a form of alternate service. The two venirepersons, who sued on behalf of a class of persons who would be present in future jury venires before Judge Guarino, asserted that Judge Guarino had violated their First, Fourth and Fourteenth Amendment rights...

"On April 8, 1992, the parties entered into a stipulation pursuant to which Judge Guarino promised not to require venirepersons who had not been selected for a jury to return to his courtroom nor to punish venirepersons without due process of law...

"Nonetheless, on October 22, 1992, Judge Guarino held a venireperson in contempt after a colloquy in which she repeatedly stated that she had moral difficulties with passing judgment on another. On November 5, 1992, the Levy plaintiffs moved to re-open their motion for a preliminary injunction...

"On November 10, 1992, while Judge Guarino was in the midst of a criminal trial, Judge Alexander Bonavitacola, Administrative Judge of the Trial Division of the Court of Common Pleas, entered Judge Guarino's courtroom and requested that he call a recess [and] delivered to Judge Guarino an order that he had just received which was signed "BY THE [PENNSYLVANIA SUPREME] COURT: [T]he Order ... assigning the Honorable Angelo Guarino to the Philadelphia Court of Common Pleas for the period of November 1, 1992, to November 30, 1992, is hereby revoked. Judge Guarino is not authorized to complete unfinished business pending before him...Since issuance of the order Judge Guarino has not been reassigned to sit as a judge, and his pending cases have been reassigned to other judges."

Nor did he ever sit again. He appealed the order of the Pennsylvania Supreme Court to the Federal Eastern District, claiming that he had been deprived of his constitutional rights by being kicked off the bench. The case eventually worked its way to the Circuit Court, which ruled against him, and he died a few months later, heartbroken at the prospect of a future in which he could never again be able to terrorize innocent citizens in his courtroom, a sad ending for a great jurist.

Afterword

So, there you have it; some stories and ruminations from my legal career. I had more, but as both your time and patience are limited, I restrained myself. You may have noticed that most of my trial stories ended with acquittals, even though I actually lost about half of my cases. Well, who wants to remember the ones that went wrong?

In any case, I hope I was able to shed some light on what goes in the typical criminal trial, as opposed to the ones reported on the news, and that you didn't have to struggle to keep from nodding off while you were reading.

I welcome thoughts and comments on this book, criminal law, and whatever else is on your mind at: aheller2@verizon.net

www.ingramcontent.com/pod-product-compliance
Lightning Source LLC
Chambersburg PA
CBHW010854090426
42736CB00019B/3449